Falling Into Place

Thomas Medonis

D~~ ~~ ~~ Gonzálz~~ C

Good Word Books

Chapter One: Discovery

Amid a clear crisp October night branches were gesticulating every which way. Leaves still scarcely remaining, held by no more than a quarter of the flora, possessed a color contrary with their origin. Through the support of a slight breeze, the scant leaves descending down to acidify the soil reflected a faint shimmer from the moonlight. A season of sustenance was clearly near end. Nature had indicated it was time for the annual Adams Farms party. For Pat Adams and his older brother Mark this day had become the most important of each and every year.

All hallows eve would mark the date for the annual Adams costume party on their family's farm- land passed down since the eighteenth century. Nearly everyone within the small town disguised themselves in an arrangement contrary to their own. The party proliferated each season since its beginning, four years previous in 1975. It was the two Adams boys, Pat and Mark, who set in motion the celebration outside of their farmhouse. In the party's inaugural year they invited every person they had contact with. Surely, friends were the only guest. It was far less populated on its inaugural night than they had hoped the night would play out. No more than ten kids were dressed in costumes. Nevertheless, it was forty acres of open space with one type of parental supervision, which needed its very own supervision.

Pat's mother, Anna, was a teacher at the local elementary school, while his father, Russell, was a small time farmer, with a concentration on one crop. Russell and Anna had inherited the land from his father, Calvin, who still lived on the farm. The old man performed more labor upon the land in one day than his son Russell did in one month.

Anna had no interest in any of these parties from the very beginning. She had thought booze was the devil, which was a substance smuggled onto the farm since the very onset. And it ran through the party just as the narrow stream has flowed behind the Adams home. Anna stayed inside the warm house for the entirety, usually joined by a handful of fellow knitters. She approached the party, and more so life, by the simple philosophy, "ignorance is bliss." Holding no concern was the only means by which she could remain in her marriage to Russell Adams.

The old barns turned out to be the most ideal of any adolescent hangouts. Two of the barns were permanently open, as they couldn't stand any doors upon the rotted out doorframes. These open barns were made of concrete and the mason Calvin had hired carelessly set the hinges. There were four barns in total on the Adams land. Three fair to good conditioned barns were in close proximity to Pat's house (two being the concrete structures), while one was on the other side of the farm closer to Grandpa Calvin's house.

The isolated barn sat behind Grandpa Calvin's small modular ranch. This red barn, with paint chips on the surrounding ground, housed all of the elder's wood, as well as his green tractor. Even being the eldest on the land, Calvin had the youngest barn.

The three additional barns that neighbored Pat and Mark's house were all accessible to the partygoers' by simply driving through the tree tunnel, up the two hundred yard slightly uphill pitched unpaved crushed stone driveway. The barns were in decent shape for another weathered twenty years, aside from the rotted wood. The most robust, aesthetically pleasing barn, ironically, was the oldest. The tall white structure would always have its double bay doors closed no matter what. Many were allowed to enter by Russell however.

The large man coveted the barn more so than his very own home. Value of the barn for Russell was only second to his cash crop.

The oldest of the barns sat directly behind Pat's house. The barn was built entirely out of native milled wood just as the farmhouse. It was Calvin who built the same home his son spent both his childhood and adulthood in. Calvin, a young man at the time, built the barn upon the existing stone foundation of an inherited dilapidated barn. Only slight deformities at the expense of nature had provided flaws following the white barn's construction. The Maple sapling at the time of construction had become a bulky figure. Some barn wood subject to weather had been eaten away at- some eight inches gone.

The sturdy antique barn had stood since the 1930's on the land Russell had received from his father. The barn, Pat viewed from his back bedroom window, had an open door for just about everyone but Russell's youngest. As a kid, Pat explored every square inch on the farm except for the interior of the white barn. The land had been in the family since the eighteenth century. The exterior of the barn was white, which was maintained by Pat annually. One of those kids, Pat was quiet, but boy was he constant. Nonetheless, the white barn stood out around the other humdrum barns.

Every year he predominantly repainted the one side of the barn he had practice jai alai upon each day- unless snow covered the ground. Extensive deterioration of the previous year's paint was caused through the wear from a dirt-covered ball traveling eighty miles per hour. Pat emphatically loved the uncommon game of jai alai more than anything else and wanted to keep his playing surface clean. The sport was foreign to everyone in town with the exception of Pat and his grandfather Jacques.

For Mark, on the other hand, a basketball hoop too was fastened upon the planks on the repainted southwest side, but the net had sat near dormant since Mark's expulsion from Pittsfield High. The only instance the hoop seemed to be used was during the fiery drunk games during the party. Every year right before the big party, Pat would be at the same point on top of the ladder, wherein loud and obnoxious

Mark would give him the same hard line, "What the hell are you painting it for, it's gonna look like shit the second you start whizzing your ball against it!"

"Well," Pat would say, "Just let me get this done, don't bother me. I'd rather have it shine than look worn down."

With the barn sitting right behind Pat and Mark's house, it gave their father easy access, inside the house, to watch Pat play the same sport his father denounced. Russell, too, had his own interest in the barn. He would use the interior of the barn with Mark to weigh out his yields, which was an area off limits for Pat.

Grandpa Calvin built the Adams' large farmhouse, presenting blue wooden shutters in 1932 into 1933. Construction of the white barn followed soon thereafter. When Mark was one, Calvin handed down the house and barns to his son Russell in 1960, soon after Russell's mother died. The move was made all in hopes of Russell benefitting from a career off the family land just as his father had. It didn't work out that way however. Calvin felt it was his duty to be so charitable, because he shared something with his teenage son that would turn him evil. Father felt great guilt in what he forced his son to read.

The other two separate barns stood on the east and west sides of the house. They were smaller in size, built of concrete blocks in 1955. They were both still very sturdy with minor hairline cracks. Nearly half the windows were knocked out of the twenty six-pane units. Within the old two-floored structures dwelt a negligible amount of extremely dry hay, a lot of old tools, large families of vermin, a lot of cats, and a lot of chickens- all to the delight of the guests unfamiliar with the lifestyle.

Surprisingly more alluring than dormant buildings, however, was a loud, obnoxious, drunk parent—Russell Adams. Even with such a minimal turnout the first party, word spread of Russell's unrestrained behavior throughout town. The persona was made very clear at the onset each and every year. Thereafter, the turnout would increase every year. Sharing alcohol, wearing underwear as a costume, playing drunk basketball with teenagers, random screaming while spraying saliva every which way, were just a few of the antics.

An unfathomable outcome in 1979, in comparison with the usual euphoria of the past, would, nonetheless, make this the final party. It should have been assumed from the start that the night would not go according to tradition, as Russell, the master of ceremonies, was absent at sundown. The partygoers began to pull in the moment the sun began to descend. In years past, Russell was the first to welcome each and every guest who drove through the gate of the fenced-in entrance as night approached. The six-four, two hundred forty pound man could not be missed. Sporting the usual black ponytail and beard, the large-gut man would be waiting with one foot on a case at the entrance gates all the while as cars pulled in. He leaned back on the opened gate with support from one bent arm while waving the cars through with the other. Russell, standing one foot atop the case, made everyone feel welcome with his intoxicated welcoming.

In years previous a vociferous welcome would be shared with each car's arrival. As familiarity grew each year, as the colossal man looked down upon each driver, Russell began to receive some sarcastic condemnation. He did not let the snide comments from the teenagers bother him too much. His main reason for the greetings was to release the spring-loaded gate behind each car as it drove toward the house. Being called a drunken asshole held no comparison to the result of letting a thousand free range chickens out of the enclosure. The laying hens were one of his two successful agricultural undertakings. The two concrete barns supplied the laying shelves and the location for roosting.

Every teenager or adult who entered the gate knew Russell was already drunk. At which point they too were just beginning to drink at the time of entry. Another reason so many enjoyed the party was that age didn't matter much. Russell offered everyone a drink on the way in- aside from those under fifteen. At age sixteen, Mark had been drinking with all his friends since the first party. Pat, on the other hand, had no interest in booze. The majority of his friends however chose to experiment with the invitation from Russell at the most recent parties.

The booze this particular night, as was the case every evening, stirred the deep anger within Russell. But this hallows eve in 1979 was different. The crispness of the ether would host the final episode. The guests obviously all looked forward to Russell's rhetoric up at the house subsequent to gate security, in which he conveyed some form of a political manifesto. "We're free from what kids- taxes, war, debt, inequality?" However, he was nowhere to be seen this evening in '79. Every car entered the open gates Mark had propped open with cinder blocks. The chickens, holding a sixth sense for freedom the moment the gates swung open, flocked toward the opening; only to move out of the way with the oncoming guests. Hence, they broke out to peck through the exterior virgin grass, only to return to roost at nightfall.

Pat, but more so Mark, had to assure all their friends that their father would arrive at any moment. Nevertheless, the moment of Russell's belated arrival, conflict immediately erupted. The arrival of Russell at last came at ten of ten, the time of the party when everyone was feeling comfort with a buzz, in which mocking each other's random costume escalated. Every genre was covered- Battlestar Galactica, various presidential rubber masks, Casper, Frankenstein, Kiss band members. Russell, however, had not been forgotten.

Russell's twenty year old son, Mark, was wearing the same high school basketball jersey he wore to every party. He never once put any effort into his attire. The story was the same every year. He told everyone he was a retired ABA star. Truly, subconsciously, he was expressing his previous superior basketball ability, which he knew he certainly still held. The highlight for the oldest Adams' boy was the annual late night drunk basketball game. It was his time to shine. Mark's team never lost, as he scored ninety percent of the points. He could score off the dribble or hit a jumper from thirty feet away- home court advantage! In years past, Russell, Mark's friends, and Mark would always be on the same team opposing Pat and his friends. Pat's team, of seventeen and eighteen year olds, offered no competition or concern during the games. The uninterested adolescents only played to appease relentless Mark.

The third party thrown, however, Pat hit an amazing thirty-foot jump shot in Mark's face. Mark was so enraged that he sought something to release his anger into, which ultimately was the lattice connected to the porch for his mother's climbing pink rose bush. Without a thought, he punched a hole into it, and didn't feel a thing.

Unquestionably, Mark's costume did fit his persona. He excelled for the Pittsfield High basketball team—standing six-four, with a dead-on accurate jump shot. He made any opponent look silly wherever and whenever he played. A team comprised of lethargic friends and Russell still didn't hinder Mark's ability.

At the previous party in 78, the eighteen and over townies, who were considered friends by Mark, would play on his team. Throughout the high school years, the same gang of five to seven kids, on certain days, would get some rowdy games in on Mark's home court. The games got crazy. The group grew quite familiar with Mark and Russell as they spent nearly every evening around the white barn to score the successful crop the elder produced.

The burnouts encircled Mark the entire party—Cliff, Seth, Tommy, and Jeb. The entire crew held the same guise— patchy beard, in need of a haircut, and a bad posture. They too put minimal effort into their costumes, but they still were the noisiest and most conspicuous of all the guests. There was never a doubt that Mark led.

Pat's peers from his high school senior class were also present in '79, yet not nearly as coarse. They were the ones who were representing the costumes of the times—Jimmy Carter was the most polarized. Pat befriended his guests through various activities. He had peers, from the nerds to the jocks. His benevolence was quite inviting. Nonetheless, both Mark and Pat's friends had something in common— they had reckless fun on the Adams' farm once a year. Anna Adams', Pat's mom, had all her usual friends over as well. A few old timers were also by Russell's side in years past.

Being a man who spawned so much elation, all of Russell's friends were also simply out to get uncontrollably lit. The large drunk was thus renowned for two things in Pittsfield, yet one of the qualities was a bit out of the ordinary for a town drunk. Obviously his bout with alcoholism brought great attention, but strangely, his vast knowledge of a previous war a homegrown Adams descendent had fought in also brought him local acclaim.

His absence at the beginning of the Halloween party brought many questions from visitors, but there was no concern for Pat, who simply answered, "He's at the Sunshine Café. He probably forgot about the party."

The drunk, sure enough, would steal the show almost immediately upon his arrival. Brief exhilaration would ensue with Russell's arrival the moment he was noticed. The young intoxicated crowd, in the middle of the stone driveway surrounded by the barns and the Adams house, were thrilled as his high beams pierced everyone. A youngster pointed out the large man as he got out of his rusty old silver truck.

In the moment of elation for all the guests a reprehensible act would change the mood rather quickly. Within fifteen minutes of his arrival, none of the Adams males, except for Grandpa Calvin, would be on the farm, away in his small cabin. Father and sons would be concentrated upon a place where generations of Adams had gone to escape. This, however, would be their final visit collectively. October 30, 1979, was the final day of Russell's life.

The end for Russell was approaching, as Pat ran a mile upon the descendants' man made trail through the neighboring forest. Occupied with pines, cottonwood, ash, and poplars, the landscape provided many obstacles for Pat in pursuit of his father. The blood draining from his nose didn't hinder maximum speed. One continuous phrase ran through the seventeen-year-old's conscience as he ran after his father: "Why did it have to come to this?"

Through much heavy breathing, Pat had reached the top of the cliff. He travelled the distance, just over a mile from the farm, in five minutes. Before this final incident, the isolated spot had stood for much more than just a cliff. This desolate spot is where Pat and his older brother would sneak away for Mark to smoke his cigarettes, while Pat would gaze across the Appalachian Trail. They were never bothered on the state land overlooking the cemetery.

With the breathing slowly returning to its norm, there was no sign of Russell atop the spot. Pat expected an enormous silhouette appearing on the moonlit cliff, but all he acknowledged was the potency of the clear starlit sky.

The moment alone atop the cliff gave Pat a feel of déjà vu. He remembered the time Grandfather Calvin told Pat that Russell's anger should be blamed on Grandpa Calvin himself. This great torture Russell held within was first molded when the teenaged Russell began to read a preserved 1812 journal written by a family descendant named Henri Adams. A journal Calvin felt he forced his son to read.

The journal's relevance quickly became evident the moment Calvin opened it. Henri Adams fought in the War of 1812 and through this experience he felt the necessity to write down his role in the mischievous war, beside all the opposition he manifested. The journal for the most part was written as a diary, aimed at expressing the grave concern Henri felt toward the young expanding government. Henri, however, did not want to share this diary with anyone during his time on earth. The seventeen-year-old Russell, however, many years since its completion, got hold of Henri's prose and greatly absorbed it.

The text had such a great impact on immature Russell, who at the time didn't know a trice of history. But soon, after concluding the journal, one of the few works he ever completed reading, Russell grew wary of all forms of government. Hereafter, he would distinguish himself as a victim.

The many deceitful bureaucratic acts committed over a hundred and fifty years prior had gravely affected seven-teen-year-old Russell. Calvin Adams would soon thereafter feel great guilt in what he had generated in his son, as he had chosen to share the journal for the greater good. An heir of Henri Adams had preserved the work to be shared and that's what Calvin did.

Calvin thought it was necessary for his son to learn all the facts on the history and development of his country. The journal served as the greatest of means for this purpose. Seventeen seemed to be the perfect age for his son to openly, maturely, acquire the knowledge of a true account of the past.

Russell, adversely, perceived Henri's words far differently than his father had. Russell's main theory contrived from his reading was that the country in which he lived had developed into a nation where public servants had become dictators for their own personal benefit. "They are paid by me to spend my money to earn more money." Words Russell repeated to any open ear.

Chapter Two: The Barn

It was a bit fortuitous that Grandfather Calvin found Henri's journal. Discovery of the heirloom occurred on the thirty-acre farmland he inherited from his parents- land passed down since the eighteenth century. This was the land Russell, Pat, and Mark too grew up on.

About a year after Calvin married Juliet in 1931, he began construction of a new large rectangular shaped two-story farmhouse. Calvin obviously wanted the area around the new stone foundation cleared upon completion of the robust house. Yet, an old barn's remains had sat behind the new building. Uncertainty arose between Calvin and Juliet as what to do with the ashes, planks, and stone that filled the blighted old crumbling stone foundation.

A decision was made between the newlyweds to build a new barn upon the refurbished old foundation. It was soon to be discovered that the barn had been burned down around 1856. Calvin's first instinct conversely had been to simply bury the old stone foundation after completing his house in 1932. "One day," the old man recollected to the teenaged Pat as they split a large cherry with a maul and wedge, "Your Grandma had a vision of a large barn behind the house that could house hay for the horses, roost the chickens, and store all the necessities."

The first undertaking with building upon the original hard-wearing foundation was to eliminate the ash, loose stone, and burnt planks within the foundation. All this was done by hand, as there were no massive mechanical claws readily available in Pittsfield in the 1930s. Calvin told his grandson Pat, "Removing the debris was the most difficult task because of all those nails."

Many minor injuries resulted with the disturbance of the old structural remains. All the planks were removed thirty feet away, in which they formed a massive bonfire pile. However, a massive fire was not the highlight for the twenty-five year old able-bodied Calvin. As he was taking out the final five planks at the very bottom of the ash-filled dirt floor, something that did not belong became visible—nearly buried under ash there sat a fireproof black vault.

Calvin, shirtless, with cut-off jean shorts on during this hot July day, immediately scattered the remaining planks and then pushed aside the mound of ash. There he saw a thick dust engulfing a safe in solid condition. He then gathered enough strength to carry the eighty-pound vault out of the remaining ash. He then put it down, gathered his strength, and shimmied it through the opening he had created with a sledgehammer. Outside the foundation, he wiped it down with his sweaty tee-shirt. The safe was now shimmering under the sun on level ground.

Under the hazy sun, facing the safe, Calvin stood with dirty sweat running down his entire chiseled tall frame, eyes burning. As quickly as he kneeled down and reached over to see how it was locked, he discovered the safe had no lock. The handle latched and unlatched freely. It only remained closed because the handle was latched. It swung open with a turn and a pull. Inside sat a deep darkness as he blocked the sun. He reached in and discovered there were two different items. One item being some form of cloth, while the other item being an old brown book that offered an unfamiliar flaky leather cover. Both hands were used to remove the safe's contents. The item made of fabric turned out to be a military uniform, in which a quick analysis ensued. He had not a clue what era it had came from, as he did not know much military history prior to this discovery.

Next, Calvin wiped his hands on his hips after placing the uniform on top of the safe in order to next thumb through the journal. He quickly recognized that it was the work of a fellow Adams, as it was signed on the inside cover Henri Adams 1812. For Calvin, the simple latch became the bridge for exposing the astonishing detailed past his descendant had experienced.

In utter surprise, Calvin realized not only was Henri Adams' well-conditioned leather journal in the vault, but the army uniform was Henri's from the War of 1812. This discovery instantly made Calvin take a step back from the safe, while holding the journal. Calvin was intrigued. From the moment he first thumbed through the journal in the summer of 1932, Grandpa Calvin told Pat his life had grown a much greater purpose. His journey truly began.

That evening Calvin began to read. And he read and read until two a.m. It was a late night for a man accustomed to sleeping by nine. The following morning he picked it up off the nightstand and brought it to the table aside his eggs and coffee. He concluded reading Henri's work that evening, not tending anything to do with the old foundation. All the information written in cursive was tight and uniformed upon each page. Nearly every page held something new and scandalous. Nothing on the War of 1812 was previously known to the young man. Calvin quickly understood Henri's motive for writing in the journal subsequent to his wartime experience- bureaucracy presenting the American expansionist policy through the creation of an illusionary scenario.

Calvin had heard of the Federalist Party, mentioned often in the journal, as the first constitutional political party, but he was not aware they were more or less eliminated as a result of this war. A fact heavily displayed in Henri's text. Calvin was especially shocked about what Americans did to fellow Americans. As he sat on the porch reading, Calvin read a powerful excerpt, "To think a country, where manipulated words conduct a man's nature more so than the very action that is performed, is where I call home."

Vast research first resulted at the Pittsfield library, a measure to which Calvin verified the validity of Henri's words, all of which were true. He then began to travel first to other New England libraries and universities. As the information was accumulating, Calvin sought more information on the war that covered vast amounts of land upon the western frontier. He travelled to other institutions located in the Ohio River Valley and even as far away as Detroit, to find rare literature on the war. This great accumulation of knowledge over a fifteen-year span that accompanied the heirloom brought a great urgency inside Calvin to share this knowledge. The first and only student would be his oldest son, even though Russell was no scholar. His teenage life consisted of comics and records. Nevertheless, Calvin decided one winter evening in 1952 to sit beside the teenager on his bed, turn off the record, and share Henri's work.

Russell, too, was open to reading the journal, and he did. He read it in one week, using every evening to read under the nightlight above his bed, as he was captivated with nearly every page. Sadly, though, after reading it, the seventeen-year-old felt he was the same as Henri- a great victim of the times.

Chapter Three: The Party

There he was. Russell finally stumbled into the party as the cool misty drizzle came down. The wide assortment of guest all easily withstood the minor saturation at this point in the evening. In certain spots the water was consistently dripping off the gutter less barn roof. With nearly everyone gathered outside the white two-storied barn Pat had repainted, the sudden appearance of the large drunk from the dark foreground brought about repetitious strident greetings.

Sluggish speech reflected the disposition everyone anticipated. "Why the hell's the gate open!" All of Mark's friends chuckled in response. They especially loved the drunk because he was always shitfaced in the evenings they visited. Teenagers strangely felt at ease around Russell, contrary to how his youngest son Pat felt around him.

However enjoyable Russell's appearance was, no one expected what would transpire next. Russell passed through the crowd in a disorderly manner paying no notice to the juveniles. Russell first glanced Pat from about twelve feet away. Father was dressed in his black jeans, black jean jacket, black boots, with his black hair in a ponytail. The youngest Adams boy would receive an increasingly sinister look with each step Russell took. In due course, Pat received the look of death the moment Russell clearly distinguished what his son was wearing.

Pat wanted to wear a costume no other would have on. Thus, he chose to wear Henri's uniform from 1812, which fit. He did not bear his brother or father's large size, as he reflected the smaller frame of his mother. He was able to easily fit into the frayed uniform. Dirty blonde Pat looked quite proper in the blue coat with red collar and cuffs.

Russell wasn't aware his youngest son knew the historic uniform even existed. Storage for the uniform persisted to be in the attic of the same white barn Calvin had rebuilt from the ashes. Pat, however, was restricted to go inside the barn. Russell and Mark, on the other hand, were free to go inside of this barn anytime.

The reason as to why Pat was told it was forbidden when he was four was that it was haunted by Henri Adam's spirit. "You have no business in there with the spirits," Russell would shout to the youth if he ever came near the barn. As Pat grew older, Russell would simply remind him once or twice a year, "Stay the hell out of there and mind your damn business!"

Mark, on the other hand, was allowed with his friends in the barn anytime. The twenty-year olds would grow so comfortable through the years that in 1979 they were over nearly every day. The group, which Mark stood out of due to his size, would enjoy both Russell's anecdotes and stash. Pat was either tending chores or making too much noise playing jai alai against the barn wall that the group of older kids would threaten to kick his ass. Russell mostly instigated the annoyance.

A wall to practice jai alai against was the only business Pat had used the barn for. It was by far his favorite sport. The main reason he chose the white barn rather than the concrete barn's was for the sake of the chickens. Pat thought it would startle them. Full access was granted to the two concrete barns neighboring his house, as Pat was responsible for the chickens and stacking the wood.

Chapter Four: Jai Alai

Jai alai was first presented to Pat by his other grandfather, Jacques, his mother Anna's father. The short, chubby, bald man was always with a smile. Even though he was no athlete, when it came to jai alai his skill and technique was flawless. Grandpa Jacques introduced jai alai to nine-year-old Pat in 1971. He was very proud of the Basque country of where he came from, as too did jai alai. Papa Jacques held a passion for the Basque game and culture that he wanted to share it with whomever showed a spark of interest.

The Basque province was very intriguing to Pat, partly because jai alai originated there, but mostly because his bloodline ran through it. The interest was something the two shared in common. The youth grew quite educated about a country covered minimally at school. One negative result of all the time he spent at Jacques's luxurious home talking and practicing jai alai was the envy it produced in Russell.

The Basque country, in the western Pyrenees, borders both France and Spain. It is a country formed by several provinces, some of which who do not consider themselves of the Basque demographic. Papa Jacques came over to Pittsfield from Barakaldo, which was in the province of Biscay, in his twenties. With first finding life difficult in the new land, he was able to find solace in one thing.

Thus, the preservation of one piece of the culture he brought to Massachusetts would take precedence until the day he died. The most significant thing he imported and kept was his jai alai equipment- a pelota (ball) and a cesta (gloved basket attached to hand). Though his passion would only spread to one other person in Pittsfield, it would be his grandson Pat Adams who would inherit the skills of jai alai.

Jacques, in fact, designed both his garage and pavement with dimensions exactly as that of a jai alai cancha (jai alai court). He would be more than pleased for all that effort the moment Pat showed interest at nine in Papa's cancha, "What is that court for Papa?" Pat had already favored Jacques' warm nature growing up, but as soon as he learned the game at the age of nine, the two were inseparable.

It was appropriate that Pat took to Jacques, as the youth's appearance had favored his mother's side of the family—short with blonde hair; while Russell and Mark favored Grandpa Calvin—tall, with black hair. However, Calvin was not husky like the other two.

Visits to Jacques' house were a common practice for Pat and Mark as children. They served as a means for Anna to have time away from Russell. Jacques figured that Pat being nine and Mark at twelve seemed like the right age for the boys to be introduced to the Basque game. As the game was initially introduced to his grandsons, he demonstrated four volleys against his garage wall, catching and releasing the ball in one motion. He then simply handed each of his grandsons' a cesta and said, "It's got to be one motion, boys." Pat and Mark then put on the cesta. Pat, having the ball in his gloved net, then volleyed the ball against the wall alongside Mark. "What a scoop!" Jacques shouted to Pat as he caught the ball flawlessly. "But see Pat," Jacques continued, "A good strategy starts with the placement of the return." Pat got the concept immediately. The ball was whizzing in and out of his basket, only bouncing once or twice. The youth never wanted to stop playing. He completely ignored his brother's involvement. Mark, on the other hand, when Jacques noticed the frozen eleven year old, had trouble releasing the ball from the basket. He told Jacques, "Papa, this is boring. Not for me."

Mark was considerably better than every other boy in town in every other sport. To him, Pat could excel in this; he didn't care. Frankly, Mark didn't think jai alai was cool. The only reason he knew of it was because it was brought up every visit to Papa Jacques'.

As Mark went back inside, it took Jacques only an additional hour to teach Pat the entire technique and rules of the game. Captivated, Pat performed a mistake filled volley against the garage wall with his grandpa. Jacques called the wall hand constructed of concrete block, with plexi-glass windows, "My Frontis". There were two other fifteen-foot walls constructed of wood, one adjoining perpendicular at the side of the concrete wall, and the other adjoining the side wooden wall, facing the concrete wall. The three walls mirrored the jai alai court requirements that were used in competition.

On the second visit following the jai alai orientation, Pat asked his mother if he could stay and practice when it was time to leave. "Jai alai sleep over mommy?"

Jacques told his daughter, "No problem. Pat can stay for dinner, sleep in the guest bedroom. I will drive him back home in the morning. We can't deny the boy. We have an jai alai player here!"

Pat didn't want to stop with Jacques after his mother left, but it came time to eat. Nonetheless, Jacques lived close enough to the Adams farm, in which jai alai practice would become routine following the sleepover. It reached the point where Pat and Jacques would play five times a week. At twelve, thirteen, fourteen, etc., Pat would make the thirty-minute trek by bike. He would sleepover if it got late on Friday or Saturday nights.

Russell, though, did not enjoy watching the two, especially his son, play a foreign sport. Anger was clear the first day he witnessed his son play the game at a family party Jacques was hosting for Anna's birthday. Jacques was waiting for Pat on the back of his estate as all the family members arrived on a beautiful spring day. It was a rare occasion that Russell was visiting the round seventy-year-old, but he could not miss his wife's birthday party. He did not wander from his consistent persona however.

Greetings erupted as Anna and her family entered Jacques home. Cousins, aunts, uncles, nieces, nephews, were all swarming the forty year old. Jacques was nowhere to be seen. His brother, Uncle Danny, crouched down next to Pat and told him, "He's out there waiting for you. You make him so happy Pat."

At this point, Pat had played only a couple times prior when Anna visited her father along with her sons. Pat pulled his father's shirt subsequent to Uncle Danny's words and told his father, "Follow me."

A smile took shape as Jacques noticed Pat coming toward his fronton with his father, in which his grandson returned the facial jubilee. Pat was extremely excited to show his father how good he was at something. Papa Jacques stood on the cancha (jai alai court) he had constructed throughout five years of labor. He held the two cestas awaiting Pat's arrival. This time Russell joined the ten-year-old as they walked downward on the pitched stone path from the house.

The court's ground consisted of fine compressed stone dust, which was located in the lowest gully on the property. Large boulders bordered the inclining lawn that overlooked the three tall walls. Russell stepped up on and looked down from the tallest boulder. With Pat's first step onto the cancha for the third time, Grandpa Jacques plainly handed him a cesta and nodded. The two then began a volley.

At the first encounter, the bulky cesta was slightly awkward for the youth, but by this third attempt it had become part of his arm. Precision reigned as he was striving to impress his father.

Pat concentrated intensely with every full body hurl to avoid a mistake, but this time was different. There was much more pressure to perform. His obnoxious father would let even the pope know if he made a clear mistake. Russell's first emotions of Pat playing were made clear within one minute. "What the hell have you gotten into!"

"Jai alai Dad. I love it!"

"Why not basketball like your brother? That game was invented right here in Massachusetts. You want to become good in some foreigner's game, the same men that tried to screw America over! What's wrong with you?"

"Russell, I think it's time you go get a drink," Jacques quietly chimed in.

In Russell's deranged rationale, he found a connection between jai alai and the journal. For some deeply-rooted reason, both bore negatively upon Russell. He turned to Pat and his father-in-law after he took a few steps up the path toward the house, and said looking down on the two, "You have no business playing this Basque game. It's from the damn French. America should have declared war upon France rather than England in 1812. Napoleon screwed us. England screwed us. Even our very own countrymen screwed us. What type of ally steals from you? And you Jacques, trying to steal my son, you should be ashamed of yourself. You have no idea about anything!"

Russell left back to the party. Nevertheless, inside the large house it seemed like nothing ever happened outside a minute prior. Russell had drink in hand and new ears to fill with his disgust.

Outside, the two concluded their forty-five minute session, in which not a word was said about Russell's conduct. The moment they took off the cesta's however, Jacques told Pat how it was. Jacques sat on the second largest of the boulders and said, "Pat come sit." Pat sat and listened. "Ignore your father. He doesn't know what he's talking about. We are not responsible for what people did hundreds of years ago. His anger is within."

Jacques then whispered to the teary eyed nine year old, "Things are going to get better." Jacques did not have much confidence in his words though.

The patient Jacques had no words for Russell the remainder of the party. Even in consideration of his conduct, Russell's opinion would not hinder future jai alai practices.

Pat would continue to visit his grandfather's house for the next five years at least three times a week, if not five. Visits were either with or without his mother, enduring the thirty-minute bike ride, even in rain or sleet, as he became a teenager. Every trip, Pat left without Russell's consent, which was not necessary, as Russell was drunk and oblivious to what his youngest child did outside the farm. Russell, furthermore, never visited Jacques again, aside from the annual Christmas Party, in which alcohol cured the tension.

Chapter Five: Déjà Vu

Pat being so young was quite confused with his father's disease, but he accepted it. The combination of Jacques and jai alai was the relief from the pain. There was a previous period of time, however, Pat truly enjoyed his father's company. When his boys were little Russell was not overtly consumed by alcohol. Great memories were created during their hide and seek games in the heavily overgrown cemetery below the cliff.

The large plot with scant gravestones served as a great landscape for Pat and Mark when they were both under the age of eight. Trees grew so large alongside graves that the nineteenth century carved stones were heaving out of the ground. Russell spent joyful time climbing up these cedars and elms for the definitive hiding spot.

Getting down the cliff was the tricky part. The three would either scale down the cliff or skid down the horizontal winding trail, which overlooked this cemetery by a hundred feet. Mark would usually scale down, while Pat and Russell trotted down the path. Customarily, the three were able to reach the site of nearly two hundred plots at the same time.

At first though, the boys had to hold Russell's hands as the three walked down the easy side trail. Mark evolved into sliding down at the steepest decline on his butt, avoiding the small evergreen saplings growing up through the rock. Pat attempted the difficult descent a couple times and made it down, never appreciating the conquer of such a difficult journey. Russell always chose the easy trek. The moment they reached the graves, the boys would count to thirty while Russell would find creative ways to hide behind nature- using trees, boulders, or reeds of a pond. These were the fondest childhood memories Pat stored within.

However wonderful the memories with his father were, one incident materialized that would permanently lead Pat to evict his own father from his heart. In the year 1975, after five years of religious jai alai practice, Jacques decided it was time to give his jai alai cestas away- to his favorite grandson, who was fourteen at the time.

Papa Jacques took his daughter aside during one of the weekly spring outings, sat her down, and despondently told her he was dying. "I got that cancer in my lungs dear. I don't have much more time."

"More than anything else," he told his daughter, "I don't want any one to grieve. I want to share the rest of my happiness with you all."

She thought it was the kindest of gestures while enduring such sad emotions. Jacques next told her he wanted to hand down his most valued Basque items to his grandson—a young man who adored them and would keep them in great condition. But first before he handed over the sticks, Anna had to promise her father she would tell Pat of his ill condition subsequent to giving him the sticks. He could not bring himself to tell Pat what was to come very soon.

There was no knowledge by anyone about Jacques's ill lung condition, clearly acquired from smoking cigarettes. Soon thereafter the talk, Pat's mother inaudibly packed the cestas in the back of the green station wagon without showing signs of her emotional state. Papa Jacques had only a week to live.

Anna kept the tears back for the silent ten-minute drive home. As usual, Pat jumped out to open the gate when they made it back to the farm. As soon as they reached the driveway and Anna parked the station wagon in front of the house, Anna said, "Pat come check out what is in the trunk."

The moment she shared the gift and said they're yours, she witnessed a reaction filled with merriment, but a question immediately followed, "Huh, I can still use them with Papa right?"

"He's dying Pat," Anna said with tears rolling down her cheek. She couldn't keep the mask on any longer.

"What!"

"Very soon son."

"Oh no."

Pat grabbed the cestas, ran up the stairs into his bedroom and locked the door.

His grandfather's condition was promptly taken in at a far greater magnitude than the happiness felt from receiving the cestas. Melancholy, Pat sat on the corner of his bed with his head down. On one hand, Pat now had the exact tools for his enjoyment at his beckoned call whenever he wanted to play at home. On the other hand, his grandfather, the man who dropped everything he was doing to accommodate his grandson, would soon be dead. Yes, Pat had come to love jai alai, but it was all the result from loving the time he had spent with his grandfather, just simply doing something.

Naturally, there was only one man who could have issue with what Pat received from his ailing grandfather. Anna whispered to her husband while he performed his slight full body sway, as the two stood at the bottom of the stairwell leading to the boys' rooms. There, Russell learned of Jacques's terminal condition and his son's inheritance of the cestas. Anna told her husband, "Give Pat some time for everything to sink in."

Russell froze in response. The knowledge of his father-in-law's condition was still not enough to accept the gesture. The moment Anna turned away, the large frame man stomped up the stairs. The door couldn't even sweep into the doorstop before the call was made for the cesta's removal. To make matters worse for Pat, the moment Russell walked into the bedroom he saw one on his son's hand.

"Get that out of my house now!"

"No problem," Pat softly nodded and walked outside.

Holding in tears, Pat immediately began whipping the ball at the side of the white barn he was banished from. Paint chips were spinning through the calm breeze. Clearing his mind of his grandfather's fate took precedence over Russell's will. A mere threat would not stop him.

Surely, grabbing a beer from the fridge, Russell saw Pat outside the kitchen window. Instantly, acknowledging the dissent, the bottle was released and shattered everywhere. A sprint toward the barn followed the pop of the screen door. There stood Russell towering in front of Pat with his hands upon his hips, "What the hell are you doing with that thing? I told you to get it out of here! You will not use this, ever, on my land. Ever!"

In a somber tone Pat answered his father's threat. "Grandpa gave me these. He wants me to use them and I will. He's going to die Dad."

Tears poured.

"You know how I feel about that sport. You have no business having those on my property."

"But Dad, Grandpa is dying and wants me to keep these!"

"You are to never use them here. I am going to burn them to ashes. Clear!"

"Clear, dad."

With that he snatched the cestas. Preposterously, Russell based the root of his anger on events that came about over 150 years prior. Obviously, Pat became disheartened. The little camaraderie he had shared with his father evaporated. It was especially hard for Pat once Jacques's spirit passed on. At the funeral, with grandfather Jacques laying only ten feet away, Pat's thoughts were only spent on Russell grabbing the cestas out of his hands. No more tears came until the resurrection.

Chapter Six: The Illusion

The destruction of the sticks was all but true until one summer night in 1977, months succeeding Jacques's funeral. It was a simple evening, Pat finished bringing water and feeding the chickens at around six o'clock on a still August night. All of a sudden, Mark came over filled with great excitement. There he stood with his arms overextended outside the chicken barn. "Dad didn't destroy the sticks! I found them in the attic of the barn yesterday."

Pat had no idea how to feel. He didn't see this one coming. Never stepping foot up into the attic of the white barn, Pat thought it was just for storage. The only time Pat ever went into it was to find one of the chickens he favored that went missing. Forever frightened, the hens were the only reason he would ever walk inside that dark, damp, cool barn. Even if his father caught him carrying out a chicken, Russell would accuse the youth of doing something else, in which case Russell would yell in the most discomforting manner. "You better not be going through my shit, boy!"

Mark, conversely, entered it often. Not as often as his father, but Mark was in there daily. Mark entertained the benefits on the second floor for the longest time, since about age thirteen. Pat was not sure why Mark had this privilege. Mark first began to explore inside the barn with his father around the age of twelve. Russell showed no grief to his oldest though. It was there on the second floor that Pat's older brother quickly thereafter habitually joined their father indulging in his cash crop.

Attempting to get Pat into the attic to find the cestas, Mark revealed to Pat that same summer evening, "Dad and I go up there to smoke the pot he grows on the farm. You have no idea, huh?"

"Seriously!" Pat said.

"Yep, and I was up there just the other day waiting for him in the afternoon. It was actually a little earlier that the time we usually meet up. While I waited up there, I went through all the storage cabinets and cedar chests. I was just looking for weed, but when I opened one chest, in the back corner, sure enough, there were your sticks. They were on top of a very old army uniform."

This puzzled Pat. Now, at fifteen, Mark at seventeen, he thought his time with jai alai had passed. His passion could only be felt by reflection of the days with Papa Jacques. Nostalgia was the extent of jai alai.

"Come, check 'em out," Mark said, as the two now stood right outside the white barn's entrance.

The decision to enter the barn with Mark was extremely difficult. Pat needed to see the cestas, but Russell was his father. The two looked at each other as Mark put his hands up and shrugged his shoulders. They then walked inside. Pat made a quick glimpse up at the string for the pull down folding wooden ladder. With a brief pause, Mark next pulled the string in order for the two to enter above. A thud came from the bottom legs reaching the dirt floor. Mark, at once, climbed all the way up, with his head and then body becoming concealed in the attic's darkness. He then popped his head back through the dark entrance. "Come up, you wimp."

Pat was standing at the foot of the stairs with both hands holding his lean on the fourth step. The young man was hesitant to begin the climb. "Dad told me the sticks were to never be used here again!"

Obedience obviously had no effect on Mark. He continued to hold his head through the threshold. "Dad lets me up here everyday. I don't think he will care if you come up and check out what's up here. If Dad really wanted to the sticks burnt, he would have done it already. Dad must want them to be used again. He saving them for you."

Curiosity set in. Pat needed to know if the sticks were really up there. Papa wanted those sticks in Pat's possession.

Pat silently asked himself, "Why did he tell me he burnt them, but he stored them away?"

Mark did not go into the attic alone. Pat climbed up behind him, and, as soon as Pat's hand reached the clean plywood subfloor, the elder pulled the string for the light bulb. A bit of shock struck Pat as to the condition of the attic. He had never seen its condition. He had expected a mess, just as the first floor appeared. It was quite the contrary however—the attic was in immaculate shape. Cabinets, bins, and cedar chests were neatly placed around the exterior of the room. A simple table with a scientific scale and two chairs were placed in the direct middle of the room.

Pat was so uneasy in this new territory that he stayed away from everything. Mark walked over to a shiny polyurethane cedar chest, opened it, and reached in.

Here, Pat. You must be happy to see these."

"Wow! I guess you're right. Dad wanted to keep them for me!"

Excitement reigned over fear. There was no consideration for the father who forbid the barn or the sport Pat loved.

"Let's play!" Pat said.

Mark grabbed the remaining cesta and followed Pat downstairs. It was such a fast game, but Mark knew how to catch the ball in the basket all because of Jacques. For Pat it felt nice to have it back on. Pat volleyed to himself the first couple whips. He then slowly served the ball off the barn in hopes that Mark would take the opportunity to catch and release. Mark soon did and performed shaky to start. With each full body throw the speed increased as paint shavings were jumping off the barn. Being super athletic, Mark finally began catching the ball more often than not, rarely letting it hit the ground or bounce more than once. He was also good at placing a tricky return for Pat. Mark quickly learned the purpose of the game, and the second Mark got it, they began flinging the ball—or pelota, as Jacques called it.

Mark told Pat after a mistake between volleys, "I wish I played with you and Grandpa."

Jacques had also given Pat a bucket full of pelotas days before he passed, which Pat tucked away in his closet, absent from Russell's eye. The ball was smaller than a baseball, made of rubber, and covered with goatskin. They were whipping the one that remained in the cesta when Russell snatched it away. They were ripping the pelota against the west side of the barn wall, avoiding Mark's basketball hoop.

Mark picked up the game quick. Scoops were easy with one bounce off the dirt. They did not play for points, as a sidewall was necessary. There were definitely some misses, but the pelota for the most part was continually flying out of their cestas. Mark was experimenting with under arm, side arm, and over head releases. Mark's basketball home court had now transformed into a jai alai fronton.

In accordance with Jacques' Basque rules, Pat understood that the game was truly played against three walls—a front, back, and one connecting side—but one wall made it much easier for the amateur Mark. Pat was used to the three-wall court Jacques specifically designed, but one wall worked perfectly for his brother. The lead paint was jumping off with each volley, but it seemed that whipping a ball against it would do the structure no harm, nor were there any windows on the west side. No paint had been applied on the structure since Grandpa Calvin painted on the original two white coats near forty-five years prior. It was after jai alai beat up the barn that Pat began his annual paint job.

Pat had no concern for what his father thought. The sticks were not burnt. The brothers played worry-free for near twenty minutes, up until Pat noticed his father looking out the house window. Nonetheless, Mark and Pat still chose to continue having such fun. Yes, Mark never bothered playing the game with Jacques before he died, but at this point he deeply enjoyed it with his younger brother. Mark smiled toward Pat the exact moment their father burst out of the house with beer in hand. "What the hell are you doing?"

Mark was no longer smiling.

Pat answered his father while holding up the cesta tightly. "You didn't burn them. You kept them. You wanted me to play again!"

Russell's face turned beet red. "I've saved them so I could sell them at a tag sale if we ever have one. They have some value to someone. Your grandfather hand-made those sticks."

"Ha! I wasn't saving them for you. The only reason jai alai is even becoming popular in America is because it involves gambling, you idiot. Don't you see, boy? The only thing that brings happiness is money, no matter how you make it! And we'll never have any. Try basketball, like Mark, it's American; that's how you make money. No one else can play basketball like us around here. Even if you think you can succeed in this sport, there is a greedier man that will corrupt you and take your money!"

There was a long pause between the three as the sun was setting.

"Papa Jacques was right about you," Pat said in a firm tone.

"Oh yeah," Russell said with a smile.

"You are worthless, Dad."

With those words, a fierce slap crashed across Pat's face. It was not of a mild nature, which a responsible parent may use to keep a child in check. This was near the velocity of a punch. Subsequent to a bent forward stumble, Pat immediately threw down the cesta and ran inside. He could still hear Russell's words amid strides, as the angry drunk turned toward Mark, *"You!"*

Rage was now focused on Mark, while Pat sat on the stairs leading up to his room and wept. It was the worse of the breakdowns he ever had on account of his father. It was uncontrollable for a few minutes. Anna was off shopping, as it seemed she was never around when Russell was at his finest.

The red finger print-cheeked teenager sat in his room the duration of the afternoon into the dark evening. Mark, on the other hand, had a much different fate. Russell and Mark had quite an anomalous relationship. The discipline was extreme.

Pat became aware of this strange bond the instant Mark told Pat their father had used drugs with teenagers in the attic of the barn. This fact only verified Jacques' assumption that his son-in-law was a total mess. An unusual relationship all started that day at age twelve when Mark was playing basketball, against the barn wall. He saw Russell moving around in the barn and became curious as to what his father was doing. "What's in all those crates Dad?"

"Something very special son. Want to check it out?"

Russell had actually been packing milk crates with some of his bulk weight that he grew. He was getting ready to distribute to the area regulars. Mark walked into ten pounds all bagged into ounces. Russell made it appear to be a wonderful thing that his oldest had discovered.

"You like what you see?"

"What's that, Dad?"

"This stuff is grown on your own land. It's harmless, a herb."

"Oh, you eat it?"

"No! You smoke it. I've been doing it for thirty years. It hadn't done me wrong."

"Oh."

"Come upstairs, give it a shot."

"I want to play basketball right now. I'm kind of scared."

"It ain't scary boy."

Not long after Mark's inquisition, about the age of thirteen, he was hooked. Subsequently, through the high school years Mark became very comfortable walking into the attic to enjoy his father's personal stash alone at any time. There was always at least a bowl pack scattered on the table. All because of this habit he discovered the cestas' hiding place. It seemed to Pat that their father didn't know Mark knew the cestas weren't burnt.

Sure enough, the one assurance Mark had made to his father, as the smoked one evening, was not to go through any of the storage containers in the attic. Mark, though, couldn't resist temptation the one-day Russell didn't leave anything behind on the table. Mark was craving. Consequently, the teenager decided to look through all the storage containers. He looked in every drawer or shelf. Bam! He paused the instant he found something that couldn't be smoked, but it was what his brother craved- the cestas he thought were destroyed.

According to Russell Adams' definition of justice, Mark deserved severe punishment for this transgression. Pat never heard the details, but as he sat weeping he saw out the window Mark being grabbed by his shirt and then pulled into the chicken barn. The two remained inside for an hour.

The first thing Pat heard, subsequent to entering his bedroom, were the footsteps of a two-hundred-fifty-pound drunk coming up the stairs. Pat knew why he was coming up. "It's my turn," he thought. There were only three rooms upstairs—Pat's, Mark's, and a bathroom. Unpredictably, there was a gentle knock.

"Come in."

It was Pat's father who entered the faintly lit room surrounded by a Bee Gee and Earth, Wind, and Fire poster. The browbeaten young man could not make out what his father was holding as he looked over his shoulder. Laying stomach down with his back to the door, Pat chose not to speak.

However, he did sit right up after his father said 'Hey Guy,' and sat next to his drained son. Russell was holding one jai alai cesta. The adolescent couldn't gauge what was happening. The last instance he had with the cesta was throwing it down, nearly breaking off the basket after he was slapped. He was under the impression it would be the last time with Jacques's stick yet again.

"Here," Russell said as he pushed the jai alai tool next to Pat on the bed. Pat could smell the skunk aroma his father would often hold whenever he came out of the barn.

"I can keep this?" Pat was so puzzled.

"As long as you don't let Mark use them, I will not object." Russell got up, turned, and left the room, with no apology. A few minutes later, Mark came upstairs with his hand and an ice pack pressed against his left eye.

"Mark!" Pat yelled from his room.

He ignored Pat and slammed his bedroom door.

And so, with that beating Mark was never the same. It was the start of his senior year a few weeks following the beating, while Pat was becoming a sophomore at the time.

The only positive thing that transpired was that Pat was able to play jai alai every day.

Yes, Russell would rant his common anecdotes as Pat practiced- "send that Basque game back to Europe" or "do you remember what I told you on how the European powers treated the Indian?"

The words, however, had no effect. Pat now knew his father as a worthless drunk. But one that allowed jai alai.

Mark, incredibly, seemed to grow more enamored with his father consequent to that beating. More time was now spent in the barn rather than practicing basketball. He had previously practiced the sport, the tall teenager excelled in, everyday. However, after the beating practice just about stopped completely.

The white barn's exterior wall, which housed the fastened backboard, transformed into Pat's practice fronton. Pat improved rapidly, while Mark was falling fast. Surely, as Mark spent little time on basketball, he began losing his extraordinary jump shot. He would still shoot around for a minute after partaking in what existed inside the barn, but he didn't put the sweat equity in that he had in the past.

Basketball had previously kept him motivated just enough to stay in school. Mark had only loved science. He was into the make up of every object. Awareness for the energy in all objects was present for Mark. He told his teacher's he could see their chakras. Boy, he could put just about anything together as well. Junior year he had a B-minus average while he averaged twenty-five points a game for Pittsfield High School. There was quite a buzz around town for his senior season in 1977.

Mark's games junior season drew great excitement. His team actually ended up winning the Massachusetts State Tournament, going undefeated. The large, powerful forward led the team in points, rebounds, blocks, and steals.

Russell was never so proud as the moment Mark extended the state championship trophy toward his father in the stands. Russell, too, was at his finest during these games. Yet, his energy was not used on watching basketball intently.

More concern was dedicated toward conversations with Mark's teammates' parents or rival parents, even random strangers, rather than the actual game. No one in the stands was safe from Russell. The same anecdote would apply to any new face. He would first open a conversation with the fact that the star player was his son. Yet, without delay after he gained the person's attention, he would share as much of his victimization rhetoric as the innocent bystander could handle.

Accordingly, ninety-nine percent of the people bothered felt uncomfortable with his extreme views on how the nation was truly formed. Even if there was a sparkle of agreement, the parent would quickly brush off Russell, "This is not the venue sir." If anyone ever questioned him, he would yell louder than the referee's whistle, "You ignorant fool!" Sometimes he even got into shouting matches with local parents who knew his condition and had no respect for a drunk attending a high school game. It was so embarrassing for Pat that he quit attending games Mark's freshman year.

American publicized sports always took precedence for Russell over everything else. The result of this philosophy made for many sports to be attempted during the Adams boys' development. Russell put an enormous amount of pressure on his sons' performance in anything American they played. Pat didn't like his father's pressure and never showed any interest.

The alcoholic's belief in a superior ability possessed by his sons' fueled the dream. Mark was average in soccer, but on the basketball court he was the star hands down. He could make shots from thirty feet away at the age of fifteen with no difficulty. Talent existed within the teen that allowed him to size up a shot from nearly anywhere on half the court and hit nothing but the bottom of the net.

Prior to the beating, he too was very excited for his senior season. He felt invincible.

Following the beating, Mark Adams had become satisfied with who he had become.

Paralleling the time in 1977–1978 there was a pop-culture movement that engulfed Mark, but not Pat. Every kid on Mark's team had a pair of Spike shoes. They were coveted by every basketball player across the nation. The shoes came in the Pittsfield Tigers blue and yellow team colors making them a necessity.

Russell rarely went shopping and was tight with his wallet, but for his talented son's performance he made an exception. The instant he was told by Mark the shoes would make him a better player Russell was sold. He thus purchased a new size thirteen for the upcoming senior season that could possibly send him to any college he wanted.

A habit in the barn, however, would catch up to the star. During the first month of his senior year in November 1977, Mark's coach, Mike Gilbert, easily discovered that Mark was selling drugs to teammates. Mark was taking some of the harvest his father left for him and sold it to teammates. The bald, skinny, non-athletic coach, clear as day, saw a transaction take place in the locker room. Coach Gilbert previously overheard talk on the court that Mark "had the best stuff around." Consequently, he chose to eavesdrop after that practice behind a set of lockers.

Sure enough, there was Mark bragging in front of everyone. A zip lock bag was held up by his index finger and thumb in front of everyone. "Who wants the goods!" A teammate scooped it up just as fast as corn finds a chicken's mouth. "Five bucks," Mark would then say.

Russell would, on occasion, leave Mark massive amounts on the table. Such an abundance of it was grown that Russell never noticed any of it missing. Consequently, the star athlete thought he could make money from it just like his father had. He advertised the herb to all of his teammates, even the freshman. Obviously, some of the players told their parents who told Coach Gilbert. Though, he didn't confront Mark that day.

Mark's arrogance inescapably would get the best of him. The day after the witnessed drug transaction, Mark Adams was immediately expelled from the team and school. His mother, an elementary school teacher for the district, and father, were called into the principal's office. Anna was torn and humiliated, while Russell, on the other hand, seemed to not really care. Russell presented a simple defense to the principal. "The kid wasn't hurting anyone. It shouldn't be illegal."

Mark told his parents he was done with schools altogether at the beginning stage of the drive off from Pittsfield High in the green station wagon. With the penalty of expulsion he was done too with basketball. Life for Mark would now continue on the same deteriorating path as his father. Both were simultaneously falling downward into the same place.

Pat, however, did not let the elder's lifestyle negatively influence his character. His mother helped prevent deviance the most since the time of Jacques's death. Pat felt great comfort in his mother. Behind her big glasses and bangs, Anna would only confide in her youngest the pain she felt with Mark's expulsion. She told Pat the night of Mark's expulsion, "Those two are heading toward mighty trouble."

Mother also assisted with all Pat's work through high school. With this labor of love, the final year of high school became easy by 1979. Jai alai, though, was still always the main focus. Since accepted by Russell, Pat continued to get better and improve every day. Pat knew it was impossible to make a career out of jai alai in Massachusetts, but other areas housed the sport throughout the country. Jai alai too was a huge venue internationally. Mark, on the other hand, completely gave up on his basketball hoop and dreams the moment he was expelled.

Nearly daily, Russell would hinder the fun while Pat was practicing. As the drunk wandered in and out of the barn he would give Pat his two cents. The same theme was always expressed—the corruption of past rulers was somehow comparable with the game Jacques passed down.

"Both had become greatly successful through crooks," he would say.

Yet in no way did Russell ever try to improve his circumstances or himself, which would have given Mark and

Pat an example for success. On the contrary, Pat wanted to improve, so he stayed away from the booze, the drugs and his father. He chose to practice daily.

Sadly, Russell never gave Pat any sort of praise like Mark had received, but it wasn't necessary. Since Jacques's death, and being slapped by Russell, Pat entirely blocked out his father. Pat didn't ask his father for anything by senior year. He would rather ride his bike five miles than ask Russell for a ride. This method worked well; things were going great Pat's first two months of his senior year. Grades were good, he had a new girl friend, and he was very popular. Nonetheless, popularity existed for all the wrong reasons—all the attention Pat received was because of Mark and his father's lore.

Pat was anticipating the annual Halloween party his senior year of '79 to be legendary, and it sure was.

Chapter Seven: The Fall

Russell finally stumbled into the party quite late. He
pushed his way through the elated crowd. Just as with all the
previous parties, Russell stood out as one of the few without
a costume. He was wearing his usual ensemble—tight jeans;
worn, black, pointed boots; and a jean jacket that could not
button because his gut was hanging out. His long black and
gray hair was in its usual ponytail, which pulled the hair

away from the departing hairline. Wrinkles engraved upon the dark complexion expressed a life filled with pain.

Pat was more than excited to see him as everyone else had been. His thought process led him to believe Russell would love Pat dressed in their descendants uniform. Russell had accepted jai alai, why wouldn't he accept the costume.

Excitement quickly dissipated however. No meter in existence could measure the ferocious rage the drunk emitted the moment he glanced at his son wearing Henri's uniform. His face read as a book which penned Pat as a dead man.

There wasn't much known about the garment, except that it was very old, it belonged to a descendant, and that it was stored in the attic. Ignorantly, even after the cesta incident, Pat went up and tried it on to see if it would fit without Russell's knowledge. It fit perfectly. As the host, Pat felt it was important to have a standout costume. Mission completion. It sure did spawn great excitement.

Confidently, Pat thought all hostility was behind the two of them since the inappropriate slap. Russell viewed the relationship far differently however. To Russell, his son's act showed the great lack of reverence his son held for his father. In regards to the uniform, in Pat's estimation, his father never mentioned any restrictions on wearing the antique.

The youngest would make matters even more portentous at the instant his father noticed his youngest. Audaciously, he mocked Russell's swaying hunchback walk, keeping his eyes shut while he rocked, which the drunk always emphasized when he was lit. Holding the look of death, he commenced toward Pat. This time Pat was not afraid, he walked toward his father at the same brisk pace. Everyone, aside from the parents inside, was quietly watching. A circle formed around the meeting point, which drew closer and closer.

"Take that shit off, you ain't no soldier."

"Dad, don't embarrass me. Not here." Pat whispered face to face.

Russell began looking up at the sky while spreading his wingspan, "You think cause you're going to graduate you can do whatever you want. You ain't shit, boy." Eyes came back down upon Pat.

With the silence, every single soul then heard Pat raise his voice. "Drunken, drug-addict loser."

Pat too was now a part of the main attraction. Unfortunately, he was soon to receive sympathetic attention. His father stepped into a punch that landed directly on Pat's nose, in front of everyone. Once again he was hit by his dad, and again ran inside, but this time his mother was present. As the case was with every party, Anna was sitting with her female friends who didn't drink. She did not want to see any of Russell's antics.

She immediately bounded up off the couch and consoled her youngest. Calmly, the bloodied son was escorted alone into the kitchen and checked to see if his nose was broken.

"Are you OK?" she asked.

"Dad did this. He punched me. I think he was too drunk to hit me hard enough to break it."

She took a deep breath while closing her eyes with her head bowing down. As the bleeding ceased she remained by his side.

"I don't think your nose is broken," she said.

All of her friends cleared out of the house. From Pat's viewpoint in the kitchen, it seemed that most of the guests had left. Mark and his friends remained away in the barn, oblivious to everything but what his father stored inside. Russell soon thereafter stumbled into the house. He first observed the blood blotches on the porch before he reached his distraught wife.

"My youngest son is worthless! You won't become anything if you continue to defy me."

"You never said anything about any uniform to me!"

"You were to never snoop through my shit boy!" Russell said.

"Get out forever! You do nothing good for this family. One son is addicted to drugs because of you, and our other son you scorn because you are jealous of him."

Shock ran through Pat from his mother's words. She had never spoke in such a nature.

"I always knew you were crazy like your father. You can't kick me out. This is my land," Russell said.

Anna began crying.

"This is your father's land, Russell. He is old and doesn't realize the man you became."

"What kind of man is that?"

"Worthless."

Russell simply turned, left, and didn't look back. He returned to the Sunshine Café. There was no return home that night. The back alley behind his daily hangout would become his bedroom for the night. The next morning, adjoining a severe hangover, he faced reality.

The alcoholic, in fact, tried to sober up after his wife's deep insult. The cheapest of hotels became home during his attempt at sobriety. He stayed in that small hollow room for a week while attending AA meetings three times a day. Only Mark was displeased with Russell's absence.

In a moment of strength, husband found the nerve to call his wife following the week of silence. The call did not go the way Russell had planned it though. Pat was standing in the kitchen next to his mother when Anna received the call. The teenager listened intently to every word of the conversation.

Anna was the first to speak out. "Our lives have been calm and free of worry since you left. I will change all the locks and never let the boys talk to you if you are drunk around us again Russ."

Silence arose.

"I've been sober for a week! I feel great!"

"A week. You think a week of not drinking can fix what you have done to this family." Anna became quite upset.

"I'm sorry. I didn't know what I did. I blacked out. Someone in town told me what happened. Please let me back."

"OK." Pat's mother hung up with a sigh. Pat then hugged the frazzled parent.

"I don't know about him anymore mom."

Undeniably, Russell was in a complete downward spiral, but could he change his direction even if he was sober? The violence he had committed upon his family would never be dismissed from their subconscious. He held deep deep demons—wrongs that could never evolve into right.

Consequently, heavy drinking followed the ultimatum. The only way he ever fixed a problem was to drown it—he never held control over his emotions. He chose to drink his usual dosage of half a gallon of vodka before he gained the courage to come back home.

Russell returned home a few hours after the call- in a drunken stupor. It was now about ten o'clock at night. Anna was in bed reading. With the sound and then sight of her husband's arrival, she jumped out of bed. Certainly she thought he would be sober, as he told her he had been for a week. A feat not accomplished since he was eighteen when the two began dating.

Yes, she told him he could not be drunk around the family any longer, but as soon as she walked over to hug him, she smelt it. Alcohol held its potency on his breath when he opened his mouth to speak. The simple recognition of that familiar scent was an undesirable sign. She slapped him. It was so potent a slap that the high school senior heard it from his upstairs bedroom and ran out to the stairwell.

Russell reacted in the only manner he knew how- he punched his wife. At the same time as Pat watched the punch from the stairs, Mark joined him. They watched the violence while their parents stood outside their bedroom.

It felt like déjà vu for Pat, recalling his own bloody nose from his father's fist a week prior. Russell noticed his boys looking down on him after he assaulted their mother. Within a second of acknowledging the unwanted attention, with blood pouring from Anna's nose, the drunk sprinted out the door he left open.

Pat, without delay, checked his mother- in a near identical manner as the way she checked him after Russell's prior rage. No grave concern for his mother's health arose as she sat back on the sofa collecting tears and blood into a rag.

Pat knew it was now time to come face to face with the monster. He left in a sprint out the door.

Mark stayed with his mother to contain the bleeding. The second his foot left the porch, Pat started sprinting in the direction he saw his father leave the porch. He had no idea, though, of what he was going to do to if he caught up with the much larger man. With no flashlight or weapon, he leapt off his toes each step. With the uncertainty that his foot may find an obstacle provided from the ground he still kept his pace. With no breach, thus far, he continued on with long strides into the dark woods- bobbing and weaving the saplings, prickers and large trunks. He could hear his father from a distance, as the great separation diminished. A drunk could only run through the woods at such a handicapped pace.

Somehow, Russell gathered himself just enough to keep a slight distance from his slim son through the woods. The two knew these woods like the back of their hands. Russell, blacked out, didn't even know at this point why he was running. He was helpless- another instance Russell held no control over his actions. But this time there was going to be a consequence.

The chase deepened into the woods, on town land. For the most part, they were running upon the narrow path, which formed over the many years of Adams trips to the cliff. A feeling of gaining on his father crossed Pat's mind. Every step was propelled from anger, as Pat reached an impossible speed.

To Pat's surprise he had to stop suddenly. He had reached the cliff. He walked that path that led to the cliff thousands of times, but this instance war far different than a stroll with his brother so Mark could smoke cigarettes. Atop the cliff, the mind was filled with scenarios. He only realized he was on the edge of the cliff two steps before he would have flown off. A sense of his location fortunately grounded Pat.

The cliff was lit just enough by the moonlight to see where the drop-off was. Panting, Pat could not see the ground below the cliff where the small cemetery stretched across. It was about a hundred foot drop. Pat could not see or hear his father either. Peripheral vision was used to uncover where his dad was hiding. The manhunt halted however the moment he heard Mark's voice approaching behind a flashlight.

"Where's Dad?" Mark yelled thirteen feet away.

"I don't know," Pat grimly said. "Maybe he fell. I chased him here. Now I can't find him!"

Pat then snagged the large powerful black flashlight from his brother's grasp. The light first illuminated the hundred-foot descent and than expanded over the gravestones. When the light reached the cemetery, Mark clearly noticed their father's limp body. Instantaneously, with not a word spoke and as fast as they could, they slid down the side of the cliff as Pat lit the way. They both made it to Russell's side at the same time. Pat shined the light for one second on the limp body before he turned it toward the gravestone Russell fell onto.

Their father was in grave condition. Mark and Pat both began to panic. "What the hell," Mark said. Pat shined the light back upon Russell. They looked him twice over while feeling every inch of their father. He was gushing blood from his head. Russell's head had bashed into the three-foot gravestone of Samuel Forsythe 1814-1893. There he lay motionless upon Mr. Forsythe.

Suddenly words came out of Russell's mouth. "No man has flown greater than your father."

Somehow he briefly survived the fall, only to lose his pulse seconds later and become limp again.

Pat then said, "We need to stop the bleeding and get Dad back to the house."

The two brothers then struggled severely carrying their father's dead body up the side of the cliff. It was the longest mile ever travelled to the house. The two were instantly covered with their father's blood. Pat was in back holding him under the shoulders walking forwards. Mark held under the knees, facing away from Russell. They dropped him only once when Mark tripped on some roots and released the large legs to save himself. Yet they managed. They reached the house.

Their mother looked terrified on the porch when she saw the three come up through the wood line. There she stood speechless, with tears rolling down each cheek. She spoke the first words, "It's all my fault. I shouldn't have slapped him. I should have known. I know how angry he gets when he is drunk. I shouldn't have pushed his buttons. Why! Why! Why dear god!"

The two placed Russell down in front of the porch.

"Mom, it's his fault," Mark then said as he pointed toward Pat.

"Shut up, Mark!" Pat cried out. "He was a very troubled man. He lived a sad life."

"If you would've followed his rules, he wouldn't have gotten so mad," Mark said.

"I'm supposed to follow his rules like you? I should've smoked weed in the barn every day and got kicked out of school and become worthless. You are going to be just like him. You're an idiot. You're disobedience is the only reason I discovered the uniform in the first place."

Pat stepped up, now face to face with Mark following the verbal exchange. Mark simply turned and stormed off into the barn, despite the fact that Russell was lying dead underneath his wife and youngest. The two stayed and wept together. "He needs to be put to rest mom."

Anna nodded.

Pat then grabbed a shovel from the barn, dug a hole behind the white barn, and buried Russell that same night. Help was not offered by Mark.

No one would ever be the same.

Chapter Eight: The Journal

A proper Christian funeral did not seem appropriate.
Anna did not stop Pat once he started digging. She was in
such great shock, but her husband had become the most evil
of men. Deep down she knew that his elimination would
bring peace. Moreover, Russell did not have any true friends
who would come looking for him. The only possible people,
aside from Grandpa Calvin, who would come looking, would
be his dope head customers. It was an unlikely scenario, as

Russell stressed the same point to every new customer, "Don't come looking for it at my house, I'll bring it to you."

Russell had no religion either, but he did have a father who lived about three hundred yards away. Calvin was indifferent as to what his son had truly turned into. He knew his son was an alcoholic, and consequently, he made the tough choice to distance himself. Sadly, Calvin felt completely responsible for Russell's disease, which may have been the deep seated reason he did not meddle.

Anna asked Pat, as he finished digging an eight by eight, six feet in depth, hole, with a shovel and pick axe, "What should we tell Grandpa?"

Pat didn't respond at first, as he was presently straining himself by dragging the dead weight of his father into the hole. The two looked down on the limp drunk tumble down into the hole forever.

The only two people they needed to provide an explanation to for Russell's burial was Mark and Grandpa Calvin. Grandpa Calvin lived in a little cabin on the far end of the thirty acres that he and his son owned. The old man was not seen much by anyone. Calvin felt alone, beside feeling shame outliving his wife. Not to mention the heartache Russell provided. But Pat visited him quite often, kept him company, and helped with many of the duties that were becoming difficult because of Calvin's elderly age. Nonetheless, Calvin tended his minimal crops and still continued to split firewood with a maul into his seventies.

Grandpa Calvin would split firewood all summer long with no shirt on. He never asked his grandsons for any help. Taking it upon himself, Pat would be the only one who ever volunteered his time to help his grandfather. The old man did everything he could for himself.

An endless raspberry patch fell in his front yard, which rested upon the chicken fence. The bare-root berry plants were planted five years after Russell took over the house. Calvin loved raspberries and decided to plant a patch neighboring his house. The entire town would come pick the juiciest Heritage Raspberries in Pittsfield every September, while simply leaving a couple of dollars in a moneybox stationed on a table. The chickens would get to the suckers that grew through the fence.

Calvin also grew numerous vegetables, which he would bring to his daughter-in-law, while also selling them by the honor system at a little farm stand on the main drag. It was comfortable living for a kind soul. As all father's plan for, his son was to continue on with the same work ethic and live off the land.

The plan was going accordingly during Russell's teen years up until Calvin shared Henri's journal. Great consequence would result with having the young man read the journal. Quickly thereafter, the little help Russell shared during the final teenage years disappeared. Yes, agriculture would attract Russell, but the energy he spent into it would be put forth into a crop that was prohibited.

Russell cleared an area far behind the house surrounded by woods a year after he married Anna in 1955. The area where he grew hundreds upon hundreds of pounds of pot was engulfed by pine trees and their saplings, denying any visibility within. He germinated his seeds from the previous year, continually growing the same potent variety year in and year out. Calvin did not venture in that direction too often, which led Russell to think his father had no idea how he made all of his money. As negligent and careless a father he was, Russell, ironically, was very responsible when it came to growing a superior product- a craft he learned from his father. Every little change made to the growing conditions led to the plants improvement- adding leaf compost, adding a little lime, making trenches for better drainage, or constructing tree rings around each plant during dry spells.

Pat told his mother, while he finished leveling the dirt upon Russell with his foot, "Let's not involve the police. Don't worry Mom. I'll also break the news to Grandpa about what happened to Dad."

Guilt could not be shaken, she again wept hysterically. "His death is all my fault. Grandpa is going to call the police and evict us from his land."

"Mom, give me a chance to fix this."

Pat woke up at eight the next morning and knew exactly what had to be done on this Sunday. The encounter wrestled with his mind all night. The two-minute stride passed the chickens, across the small stream, around the raspberries, over the dilapidated stone wall, to Grandpa's house, was filled with uncertainty. During the walk, Pat envisioned Calvin working on his woodpile without the slightest idea that his son was dead. It was certain Calvin was already up and working. Still, as Pat passed the vacant enormous pile of wood in front of Calvin's cabin he had not seized any specific words to use on his grandpa. Pat had no idea how the reserved farmer would take the news.

The daily labor for the old man this time of year consisted of pruning raspberries and stacking wood. However, Calvin was nowhere to be seen outside. Pat knocked on the door of the small wood cabin, but received no answer. He slowly opened the door and yelled, "Grandpa."

Pat heard a faint "Yep" come from the opened basement door, which truly stirred the nerves of the seventeen-year-old. Pat then heard Calvin's footsteps gradually draw near from the five-foot high basement up to the ground floor. "It's getting cold, time to burn some wood," the old man said, coming up the stairs with a smile.

"I know, I have been filling the wood stove all week," Pat said.

They now were standing face to face. He looked very happy to see Pat. Not a worry in the world.

"Where's your dad? I haven't seen him in a couple days. I got a bunch of extra oak for you guys out back," Calvin spoke still in his long underwear.

"Grandpa, that's why I'm here," Pat said.

"He get arrested? That drunk will never learn."

Calvin was a sharp old man, still baring a full head of short white hair. The elder Adams found great amusement in what Pat was going to tell him.

Pat had to be blunt nevertheless. "He's dead."

Grandpa Calvin dropped to the chair a few feet to his right. "I knew this would be his fate—dead before me! How?"

Pat would tell him every detail of the Halloween party, including the use of Henri's uniform, and all the events that followed.

Pat concluded, "Mom feels awful guilt. But, it was my actions that caused this, grandpa, not mom's. We ended up burying him next to the barn."

Silence filled the old man for near thirty seconds. Eyes closed, with a slight repetitive nod, was the manner in which he accepted the news. To Pat, this was the first moment Calvin appeared withered.

"It's only right that's where you buried him- next to that damn barn. That's where I found that journal you know. And that journal is what first troubled your father's mind. He never tried to make things right after that first reading. Listen to me Pat, I know he treated you guys like garbage. If anyone is to be blamed, it is me!"

Pat interrupted, "He had a disease. He actually went to AA meetings last week, Grandpa."

"That boy's been to a hundred of those meetings, but he never wanted to change his mind. He's always felt as the victim. It made me sick that he told you the barn was haunted. Do you know how hard I worked to build a sturdy barn for the generations to come? I simply told him that barn held many spirits, all because, to me, that hardback brought a dead man to life. Yet, he manipulated my words to make the barn seem evil. It was Henri's spirit that inspired me to construct such a sturdy barn, but it was Russell's spirit that made me no longer want a part of it! I have truly parted with my son quite long ago Pat."

Pat tried to sway his emotions, as his grandfather began to weep in his own hands.

"I was never allowed in there, but Mark is in there often," Pat said.

"He's turning into your father. He's addicted to dope! I see everything from over here. Your father grew hundreds of pounds around here and sold it all over. He jeopardized the land our forefathers have bled and sweated for. But I never said a word. That dirty business is the only way he was able to buy the booze. Your mother don't give him a dime from teaching."

"I had no idea until recently grandpa. I had no idea you knew about all of this either. I suppose it was only a matter of time before things caught up to him."

"Yes my dear boy." Calvin collected himself as tears running down his cheek, "I knew he was on the wrong path the moment he finished reading that journal. I had to take it back from him. He thought this world was no good, that it is based on corruption, war, and legal enslavement through debt. He told me the day after he finished the journal, 'bureaucracy was the only victor in war, and it was war that imposed a subjugating debt altering true human freedom. Countryman did not care for fellow countryman. There was no belief in a universal good.'"

"I heard it all grandpa," Pat said.

There's no denying he made a lot of sense Pat, but he became so damn angry."

There was silence for a stretch.

"Do you still have the journal?" Pat asked.

"Yes I still have it!"

"Can I see it?" Pat asked.

"Well. Pat, you are different from your father. I know this. It would be unfair to deny something that was intended to be passed down. I think it may work for you as it had for me, but promise me one thing."

"Sure. Anything, Grandpa."

"We are all here to make this world better. We must overcome hardships and learn from the difficulties, always remaining humble, as you are now discovering. This is how we learn and grow. With this knowledge, we must first improve ourselves before we attempt to fix anything within the exterior of our souls. No one is superior to another. We must stop judging based on differences. Everyone has something to share Pat. Understanding the whole is intelligence. Will you do your part?"

"Of course. I know I have a lot to learn," Pat said.

A visit to share the death of Calvin's oldest son had now turned into a moment of definitive growth, which Pat intended to continually increase. The old man slowly got up after the promise and went into his room. A minute later, he walked back into the room Pat was standing and handed over the heirloom journal. The teenager noticed a piece of paper sticking out.

"Here it is. Keep it. The piece of paper describes why the barn was burnt down, but everything else was written by Henri."

He handed Pat the leather-bound journal enclosed by a rawhide strap.

"Wow. I will try to make things better, Grandpa."

The old man stood up and walked to the front door, wherein Pat followed. He gave Pat a huge hug- the first one he ever received from his grandpa.

"Just use it for good. It's all yours son. And don't feel any responsibility about your dad. I'll talk with your mom—she'll be fine, just shaken up. Mark, however, needs to learn a lot for himself. If you need a place to stay I have an extra room. I'll put you to work to make some money—but go now, I need some time alone."

"Of course, I'll let you know what I think about the journal though. I'm going to get going."

"Take care."

Pat walked out of his grandfather's house stunned. The visit went nothing as he had attempted to envision. Pat now held a historic artifact that described an era he knew nothing of. Never before did he think history was of any importance, but this wartime journal held great significance. A family member wrote it long ago, and however impressive the old journal was, it still caused great misery for his family. The least he could do was give it a shot to understand why.

Chapter Nine: Dissent

Russell demonstrated the power history holds upon our minds, which brought on the strong curiosity within Pat to discover the journal's contents. The year 1812 had no significance to Pat until this point, apart from bringing so much rage in his father.

The heirloom was opened the moment Pat reached his bed following the sanguine encounter. Now that Russell was gone the house was silent. Shocking to Pat, was what great condition something produced in the early nineteenth century had held—some handwritten cursive was faded but still legible. Pat randomly turned the pages, reading a sentence or two from each page. Subsequent to skimming a page, he reached the individual piece of paper sticking out about two-thirds of the way into the journal. Lying on his stomach, knees bent, feet in the air, he read the one paragraph written upon the unattached paper:

> *Thank you for finding this journal. Please read it, discover the past, and share it with the future. Henri Adams was a great man and father. He wanted to share his story with anyone who would listen. Henri was a man of truth who fought for the country's most proper motives—Peace and Freedom! He passed away in the year 1856 of a strange disease. My father did not want anyone to contract the illness, thus he was cremated in his home. I felt this journal should be shared as my father shared it with me. Hence, I stored it in the fire safe in the groundwork. Pass this on to your children.*

Henri Adams Jr. 1856

The note brought Pat relevance with the past. More importantly, it gave him an idea of where the journal came from. Curiosity was stirred. He next thumbed back to the beginning. The opening described why Henri chose to write:

As we sat with Father by the fire every clear night, the stars' spoke. Cruel stories of our fathers were stretched through the evening's hours. A relative, Obadiah Adams, having lived through New England's most violent war, was spoke of most often. Obadiah was born of an Indian mother and a white father. Stories from the war in 1675, between red and white man, ran clearly across the evening sky. The white man would eventually win, in which the Indian would lose his homeland. Obadiah would flee Springfield west to Pittsfield, which defines my present location. Having heard hundreds upon hundreds of different stories on different tribes and sachems, the night has come to please me most. The tales under the sky were far different from the stories I heard from most everyone. As fate would decide, I am now involved in war too. By some means, the battle for supremacy by the world powers has pulled me in. Now, time has come to share another

story.

Reading the first paragraph was all Pat needed. He was drawn in for the entire journey. Being that the content was on relatives centuries ago, the entire work was most rousing. The journal recorded thoughts and occasions, but Pat would discover it was more than just a diary or memoir. It was a political voice that described Henri's enlistment as well as his opinion.

Expressions of an ill opinion on the injustice that brought him into the theater of war are expanded upon in text after his time in the service. Pat was soon to discover that the turn of the Eighteenth Century was a time for political transition. The revolution had ended, while remnants of distaste lingered within political ties. Dissent toward the new political system of America would naturally ripen. Just as a young nation conquered its unjust mother, a new breed of politicians sought to conquer the political stage. A collective effort by political parties grew partisan clout through conquering land. The expansionist conquest ultimately became the voice for the majority of the people.

In 1800 the most influential of all elections took place. This election would not favor the overall well-being of New England, as Thomas Jefferson's win over John Adams brought financial independence for the procured American debts of France. The obtainment of vast western land, especially the Louisiana Purchase in 1803, prescribed to the ideology of expansion. Pat read in an early journal entry, "A philosophy forever to hold precedence in America." Originally, France held the enormous allotment of Louisiana before America spent fifty million francs and cancelled numerous debts. The transaction clearly sustained the kinship between President Jefferson and France.

Henri made it very clear that the result of the prior presidential election of 1800 is what truly planted the seed for the Louisiana Purchase. An ominous political landscape grew within the young nation. It was the first time in America one political group peacefully transferred authority to another group, which occurred because of one major clause. A compromise of the Constitution formed a measure in which each slave, already considered as property, would be fractionally considered a citizen. Moreover, a servant was factored in as three-fifths of a citizen, therefore requiring representation from Congress. Yes, slaves held a vote to elect a proper representative. However, a slave being property of an owner relinquished his rights to his master. Biased voting occurred, as well as an influence on the levying of taxes.

This constitutional measure gave slave-populated states an increase of representation. As new states arose with this formula, the hierarchy held a greater power to elect their own and influence officials, which consequently formed a new majority. This constitutional measure undoubtedly developed policies a slave owner would best benefit from- a measure that has distorted American politics forever.

Reading this material brought upon much nostalgia within Pat. Russell's words "Hypocrisy is our democracy," stuck inside Pat's mind as he read.

All very fascinating, Pat began to understand his father's opinion toward the establishment. Pat reasoned that men who built wealth enslaving and abusing human rights obtained greater political clout than a man who tended everything fairly.

Thus, the Federalist Party, authors of the Constitution, lost its majority in Congress for the first time with John Adams's loss to Thomas Jefferson in 1800. If slaves were excluded from being counted in voting, the Federalist John Adams would have beaten the anti-Federalist Thomas Jefferson. The southern voters would have lost fourteen electoral votes, and Adams should have slimly won 63–61.

Adams, politically, did not side with France in the European world of conflict, and he held little confidence in England. Jefferson, on the other hand, was in France when the royal Bastille prison succumbed to the revolutionaries in 1789. "The revolution of France has gone on with the most unexampled success," wrote Jefferson to Madison.

Jefferson, Henri made clear, was quite intrigued by the course of the French uprising. In France, he discovered that anger existed deep within civil people, and consequently, the political tool of illusion held the power to lead evil energy into physical form. Jefferson, moreover, held "remarkable tenderness toward France, because that power controlled Spain, from which Jefferson was eagerly seeking the cession of West Florida."[i]

The republicanism sought by Jefferson compared with the republicanism sought by the Federalists would become "a war of principles," according to Henri. The Federalists felt the necessity of a community based system rather than one benefiting an overlord. Adams' loss, however, nearly surrendered Federalist impetus. This notion for superiority would mold a society that craved material, popularity, land, and gold, rather than developing ideas for the greater good.

Sectional consciousness began to stir in the political minds at the time of Jefferson's presidency. At times, both Federalists and Democratic-Republicans (anti-Federalists) would unite against those who disavowed territorial expansion. The Federalist Party would dispute acquiring new boundaries, as they largely represented the interest of the northern established section of America.

Chapter Ten: Impressment

The law of attraction enthralled Pat just within the first few pages, just as Russell was sucked in.

The Federalists had to continue to act with vigor; for thousands of rich federalists have tasted the sweets of monopoly, desirous of continuing to reap its advantages, [and] will give [non-federalists] votes. This is the frailty of human nature; but as a party, they must act consistently. Let our question be, are you for the poor, peace and commerce; or the rich, war, and speculation.[ii]

There was a great deal of emotion within the journal, which made for a captivating read. Henri made it very clear that The War of 1812 had everything to do with foreign interest and expansion. Moreover, Pat had already assumed from his father's rants that harm would be committed upon America through both France and England after Jefferson's election.

Henri, in his early entries, elaborated mostly on foreign affairs and the relativity they had on forming the war he was to engage in. France and England, at this time, were in a great conflict. Both were yearning to become the superior world power. Britain, consequently, was also being harmed at the time by her offspring, as Jefferson favored the prospects France promoted.

Together with a rapid growing nation, a great necessity for new American ships grew in order to distribute goods and defend the coast from the great maritime threat of England. In 1793, well manned British ships held their greatest number of regularly bred seamen ever possessed. It was at this point of superiority, consequently, that the maritime power became infamous. However, inattention to develop regularly bred Englishmen at this time of prestige, as well as, the rise of the merchant class and the lack of the Navy's discipline, led to the decline of the British seaman.

One thing not considered by the American public in this time of impressment was that Englishmen were subjected into their own Navy. The ill treatment that subjection provides thus brought on desertion. Large numbers of Englishmen therefore fled to America for familiar opportunities. England, however, still felt they had every right to their English-born American belligerents and neutrals. Nevertheless, it was impossible to stop men from leaving. Wages rose from eight to twenty-four dollars a month. British sailors began to desert from every privateer and frigate that entered American ports. Great Britain was aware they could not recover deserters on land, yet they knew they could retrieve them on the sea.[iii]

"At first an honest attempt seems to have been made to distinguish between the men of the two countries. But the moment desertions began to become numerous, the moment the United States began to protect and encourage deserters, that attempt at discrimination ceased, and impressment grew more and more rigorous, till at last the officer who searched an American ship laughed at protections and naturalization papers, differences of language and differences of race, and took off with him such men as pleased his fancy, and cared not a rush where they were born."[iv]

The matter of the impressments of sailors was one of the first things Henri wrote upon, as that was the justification for war in 1812. The removal of one man from his home country into a tour of duty for a foreign nation greatly angered him. This practice ultimately became the main pretense for declaring war upon the powerful English. Henri wrote on the matter:

> *Removed from the very land they call home, these men had been laboring to support their families! There are many men amongst us who choose for a better life here, and I am no king to deny him the prospect, but, at times, loss does accompany a gamble. Impressment has cast a shadow on the laws of all nations.*

'No nation but the one he belongs to can release a subject from his natural allegiance, as that, provided the jurisdiction of another independent state be not infringed, every nation has a right to enforce the services of her subjects wherever they may be found. Nor has any neutral nation such a jurisdiction over her merchant vessels upon the high seas as to exclude a belligerent nation from the right of searching them for contraband of war or for the property or persons of her enemies. And if, in the exercise of that right, the belligerent should discover on board of the neutral vessel a subject who has withdrawn himself from his lawful allegiance, the neutral can have no fair ground for refusing to deliver him up; more especially if that subject is proved to be a deserter from the sea or land service.' (The Naval History of Great Britain, *by William James, vol. iv, p. 324 1837)*

America was rather welcoming of British defectors. "After five years residence within her territory, and after having complied with certain forms, became one of her citizens as completely as if he was native born. ... Great

Britain, however, contended that her war ships possessed the right of searching all neutral vessels for the property and persons of her foes."[v] America resisted. Great Britain pursued their defectors using the system of impressing sailors, "by which men could be forcibly seized and made to serve in her navy, no matter at what cost to themselves."[vi]

In terms of maritime rights, the United States asked only to have its own trade respected by all nations. Napoleon Bonaparte of France, however, would not consider America as a neutral. Bonaparte had, in fact, employed the most severe methods to exclude the British from trade. Notwithstanding Orders in Council and blockades, British licenses had been approved quite liberally in order to permit American vessels, holding false papers, to land British goods throughout the world, wherein they could be smuggled into central Europe.

Aside from the great dangers, this proscribed trade augmented wealth for both carrier and shipper. British manufacturers thus increasingly practiced such means that the American flag was 'prostituted in the north seas of

Europe'. All parties vested in the Baltic trade knew well that nearly all of the English ships, travelling into the ports of Russia, Denmark, and Sweden, sailed with false papers and under American colors. Several of the powerful nations had protested, and Napoleon, moreover, declared that the illicit trade practices should halt. Thereupon, French privateers plundered the northern seas with little restriction.

England and France had come to destroy American foreign commerce, as each was fulfilling their own interests. However, France, when pressured, had supposedly ceased their deviant ways upon the seas, according to the injured American nation. England, on the other hand, likewise pressured, wouldn't halt.

French rationale foretold that the plunder of a neutral in times of war served as a means for survival. Meanwhile, England's injuries upon America were of a much greater magnitude as the British dominated the sea. Napoleon's Milan decree "declared that any neutral vessel which permitted itself to be searched by a British cruiser should be considered as British, and as the lawful prize of any French vessel. [Thus,] French frigates and privateers were very apt to snap up any American vessel they came across."[vii]

In 1807 the British fifty-gun ship named the *Leopard* would attack an American frigate, the Chesapeake, and this incident would stir great anti-British sentiment. The American government would soon thereafter place an embargo on all foreign trade during the duration of the Napoleonic Wars (1803-1815). All intentions were to avoid war and property damage, but most importantly the embargo indicated that American neutrality was violated. Consequently, the intention for economic strife upon the belligerent European nations backfired more so for one particular section of America. It was the New England states most crippled by this halt on foreign trade.

Henri made it quite clear that he did not favor the embargo.

We were subjected to an administration, which began a system of commercial restrictions, which they said, would not only prevent effectually, the necessity of war thereafter, but would put us in the quiet enjoyment of the rights and advantages we sought to establish. We have, since that period, witnessed, under the embargo, non-intercourse, and non-importation systems, a continued and rapid decay and destruction of our commerce and prosperity.[viii]

Hereafter, on May 16th, 1811 an American frigate named the *President* wrecked a British sloop named the *Little Belt*. This deadly battle was the result of an incident fifteen days prior on May 1st- the British impressment of an American named John Diggio, of Maine. The apprentice sailing master was aboard a brig, the USS Spitfire, off the New Jersey coast, when the English frigate, the HMS Guerriere, stopped the Spitfire and impressed the Maine citizen. Upon such a bold act, the Secretary of the Navy thereafter ordered the President to patrol the Atlantic coast from the Carolinas up to New York.

Little Belt was spotted at noon on May 16th, in which the President pursued. Late into the night, past ten, the two ships were now in hailing distance, wherein the two captains requested the other to identify their ships- both refused. Soon after the proper etiquette a shot was fired, thus beginning the battle. The Little Belt stood no chance as it was a much small vessel bearing twenty guns to the Presidents forty-four. Eleven of the English were killed on board the Little Belt, while not one American suffered a fatality. Thus Great Britain "issued her Orders in Council forbidding American trade with France,"[ix] as the French were an enemy to England in wartime.

An additional loose piece of paper had found Pat the instant he turned to the page where it had been folded into. Found nearly a quarter of the way into the journal, the paper was an actual newspaper article from Henri's time. America's greatest concern was portrayed, which was not stirring upon the seas. The small triple folded newspaper article was from the *Palladium* written January 28, 1808:

> *In an interview with a person who just came from Detroit, "He states that the prevailing opinion in the*

British settlements [of Canada] in the neighborhood is that there will be a war between this country and Great Britain. In corroboration of this opinion he states that there are now at Fort Amherstburg, a British post about eighteen miles from Detroit, at least 2,000 Indians, almost exclusively warriors. That they are all armed, and supported at the expense of the British, and with great liberality.... In case of war, it is expected that, under the auspices of the British, a general massacre will take place, for which they are held in readiness.

Yes, Jefferson first chose economic sanctions rather than armed conflict during his final year as President, but war would soon inevitably follow. By 1811, with James Madison as president, American politicians from the west and south, defined as the War Hawks, were in control of the House of Representatives. These men were young, arrogant, and eager for war, but yet they knew very little of it. Certain northeastern men of a particular ideology also favored war.

The question was, which nation to declare war upon? It was decided that America could not do France harm.

America would have to stretch too far to fight France. She also had no commercial value on the ocean, nor had she any neighboring possessions America coveted. America had already received from France the 828,000 square miles for the Louisiana Purchase in 1803.

The answer for whom to attack would be found upon the northwestern frontier. A prolific economy had sprung between Europeans and the Indians on land yet conquered by budding America. The allied tribes had long been compensated with ammunition and merchandise from the strategically placed forts placed in desolate areas. Thus with the assistance of the Indian the Europeans safely held their bounds.

American politicians, on the contrary, assumed that if they were to conquer the northern frontier, they would reap the like benefits as that of the Europeans. Meanwhile, the Indians and white compatriots, who retired in the wilderness, had continued to hold the same opinion instilled by the French Canadians during their surrender of Canada in the French Indian War, that the American's held designs against their freedom.

Thus, with the consideration of England's maritime force, their impressments of American sailors, and their neighboring domain in Canada, President Madison declared war. Some bureaucrats sought the expulsion of the British from Canada altogether. An additional belligerent also spawned great attention, which the Indian played in all developing American areas. In consequence, the Indians would play a crucial role in conflict. The large Indian population that lived between Canada and America were more or less neutral. Henri wrote an excerpt from the British war minister's words on the undefined relations between America and the Indians:

> *I certainly concur in your position, that attention must be kept up to conciliate the Indian Tribes upon the following Principle: that if in a contest they are not employed to act with us, they will be engaged to act against us, and that we are to consider not so much their use as allies as their destructiveness if enemies.*

I shall therefore be ready to support the temporary arrangements you may find it necessary to make in this view.

Should an amicable adjustment take place with the American States, it is possible that some joint system as to the treatment of the Indian Nations may be agreed upon, which would form the basis of a permanent arrangement with them.[x]

In 1812 many factors presented themselves as justification for war—anything from envy for the British fur trade to the trouble on the Atlantic—but paramount to all, was the British alliance with the Indians on the northwestern frontier, which hindered American expansion. There would be, however, a few political resolutions prepared in order to receive enough consent for war. A pledge was made between the northern and southern men who would vote in favor for war: "We consent that you may conquer Canada; permit us to conquer Florida."[xi]

Madison, his Democratic-Republican majority, along with some Federalists, who favored the war, declared war on England. Most northern Federalists, however, strongly opposed, as they felt the Non-Federalist administration deliberately ruined its commerce and prosperity. "Holding these views, it could see no worse national crime than a war against England which would render indirect aid to Napoleon [France], and no worse disaster to its own interests than a form of expansion which would mean new states to increase the Republican strength in congress."[xii]

The estimate cost of war was $10 million. "To meet the fixed charges and the accruing interest on new loans, they proposed an increase in the import duties which should bring their yield up to 6,000,000, and internal taxes to the amount of 5,000,000."[xiii] Cognizant politicians, though, feared that the American people would be burdened by both higher import taxes and an increase in cost for nearly everything.

Governor Griswold of Connecticut presented another matter of opposition. He expressed that the president's call upon the states' militia was unconstitutional. President Madison declared war on June 18th, 1812, but for the militia to be constitutionally called upon, he needed one of three things to occur: invasion, insurrection, or the necessity to execute the laws of the United States—none of which were applicable at the time.

At the time of the declaration of war, four thousand men had been recruited, while the total force did not exceed ten thousand. Men who were scattered all throughout the country in twelve garrisons they could not leave. In April, Congress authorized the president to call out one hundred thousand state militia, and then in June, no one knew whether all the states would regard the call, and still less whether the militia would serve beyond the frontier.[xiv]

Awareness for Henri, of all the political affairs involved with war, began during the time he served as far west as Detroit. It was written that he would not have volunteered had he known his sacrifice supported zealous expansionists-Men who used the taxpayers to expand their political clout. The twenty-year-old volunteer later wrote, "Great ignorance sat inside when I joined." Henri learned swiftly from his peers, the existing New England servicemen, on the true business of war.

Pat read an excerpt on the matter of his enlistment:

"Love of country had determined my fate. Tis the greatest necessity that I sacrifice the arduous, but fruitful life. A fight for our maritime rights and the freedom I hold must commence. Freedom, possible for all because of a previous revolution. We must not go back to those days. We must stand united. If men are taken from the sea why would they not be taken from their farm?

Henri, however, would quickly change his desire for the war as soon as he experienced the real thing. He was sent to Detroit to fight Indians and the English. There he withstood mass confusion by his own General. Questions increased amongst his comrades, as to the validity for the declaration of war based on the impressment of sailors.

I did not know that I would be involved in a conflict for Canada. I must admit I was fooled. 'We were told that

the voice of the people is for war. But the present
administrators of affairs will find before the year ends
that they have sadly mistaken the voice of the people.
That voice is not for war. It is loud for peace.'[xv]*"*

Henri was one of a handful of souls in New England who volunteered their service. Men from other states, however, served in great numbers. Alongside Henri, men from far-stretching states held various accounts as to why they chose to fight for the United States.

"After the declaration, in the States where the war
was popular, or fear of the Indians pressing, the ranks of
the volunteer regiments began to fill. But in New England
every expedient had to be resorted to in order to get
soldiers. Then was it [made] that men who had made up
their minds to stay at home had tempting offers made to
such as would go. The Republicans of Newtown, in
Massachusetts, agreed to pay any inhabitant of the town
who would volunteer four dollars and fifty cents per
month while in the field. Roxbury voted to raise the pay of
her citizens serving in the army to fifteen dollars per

month. ... [Outside New England] at Lexington the bounty was six and the pay ten dollars.

This made the war fever rage so fiercely that a draft was necessary to determine who should stay at home. In Kentucky, popular as the war was, the Legislature thought it prudent, in order to keep troops in the field, to give each volunteer seven dollars per month in addition to the five paid him by the United States.

Where the war was unpopular these inducements accomplished nothing, and it became plain that the chief dependence must be the militia. But when, in accordance with the law, the Secretary of War issued the call for militia, the Governors of three New England States flatly refused to obey."[xvi] The three things necessary for a call to the state's militia were not occurring—invasion, insurrection, or the necessity to execute the laws of the United States.

Chapter Eleven: Time to Move

The Siege of Fort Detroit, August 16th, concluded through the capitulation by the American force within Fort Detroit. General William Hull, in command, felt the Americans could not hold or withstand the British and Indian force, which comprised of over thirteen hundred warriors- five hundred and thirty were Tecumseh and other first nation Indians.

In a short time, the British troops marched into fort, with gen. Brock at their head. We were then ordered into an adjoining garden, where the articles of capitulation were read. During the intermediate time, the American flag was pulled down, and the British ensign hoisted in its place. The batteries then commenced firing a few de joye- the Indians raised the yell of triumph, and discharged their pieces in the air. Our agitation had now reached its acme- Sullen bursts of indignation disturbed every bosom, and where tears did not flow, it was because, "Grief drank the offering, ere it reached the eye."xvii

Shamed, Henri and the American troops were removed to Montreal as prisoners. Then paroled to return home. The experience was a nightmare.

Disgrace! Disgrace! Disgrace! Poor, weak and pathetic, my vermin soul! No action could I take. Surrender was our stance and that was all to be done." Fortunate for Henri, a return home to Pittsfield followed the ordeal.

'Amid the tears of his men, it is said, and without consideration for the honors of war, [Hull] surrendered not only Detroit, with its garrison and store, but the whole of

Michigan.' Deep resentment was thus stored deep within Henri accompanying his return home to New England.

Finally home on the farm, Henri could not avoid all the war dissent, speculation, and misinformation. The literary work of several Federalists, along with New England newspapers, would be the first sources to bring confusion and dissent upon this young man. The one solution to easing his grief would be found in writing it out. Any moment Henri had any type of thought relating to his experience he would write it down. "Pain from war has evolved into a work for peace."

In regards to General Hull's conduct, Henri was torn. Henri did mention that prior to Detroit, "Hull clearly performed questionable conduct the moment he omitted to advance onto the bridge seized by the American force. This circumstance allowed the English to collect and combine their force against our force adjacent to the bridge. Whereupon, soon thereafter, we could not maintain the bridge or penetrate the English barracks, so we retreated." Henri could not deny there were flaws in Hull's leadership.

At the desk in Pittsfield it would be revealed months after the campaign that the whole Detroit operation was a great folly. The government did not consider the past experiences of the revolution as to the necessity to keep stores across such vast wild country. Hull, a veteran of the revolution, was wary on the matter of food and gun surplus. But the humiliation Henri had earlier felt would change. Anger was no longer directed at Hull for his lack of effort. Rather, he felt all accountability should fall upon the ill natured government who forced war against a mightier nation.

The art of journalism was painted by a steady hand back home for Henri. The revelation was molded that the lack of appropriate measures by the government for a successful invasion of Canada hindered any victory in Detroit. This sobering recognition brought the greatest of anger within Henri. The American force was a sitting duck in Detroit. But even more rousing was the true pretense for the invasion of Canada.

At first, it appeared to Pat that Henri was mad at a general, who held petty rank compared to that of a president. The growth of Henri's knowledge on the deep seated intentions of bureaucracy was evident through his literature. The message was clear for Pat. "It was Jefferson who truly neglected the army!" as Henri wrote.

When Jefferson was elected, he found four thousand men in the Army, but he would soon cut it to 3,200. Henri wrote, *"Jefferson was one of the many politicians who didn't participate in the revolution and instead labored as lawyers and scholars, ignorant of military affairs."*

Henry would quickly come to blame men of a much higher standing than Hull. The men who declared war put Hull, Henri, and all the other men standing ground in Detroit, in such a dire predicament. The journal reflected such a lack of communication as to when the declaration of war was declared and what the objectives for the invasion of Upper Canada were. Two things the declaration did do were increase taxation and increase anger toward the British and Indians.

As he began his journey back home to Pittsfield, he determined his preference was to tend the sheep on the family farm, rather than hold a gun. At home the great effects of this war were immediate. He wrote, '*The internal taxes, the land tax, license tax, stamp tax, carriage tax, sugar tax, and tax on distilleries, were hastening as fast as our worst enemies could wish, the destruction of these remote industrious excellent counties. What the enemy had spared, the protector, our own government, seizes!*'[xviii]

Each individual journal entry would span a greater length of time the longer he remained home, as he began establishing his own land. More time was spent on labor than writing. Writing, nevertheless, was still of greatest necessity. Most time was spent on clearing the land neighboring his father's farm within a year of his return from Detroit, which was also well documented in the journal. However, Henri would continue to share political perspective until the day he died. Bureaucracy captivated Henri as it would later influence Calvin, Russell, and now Pat.

Dissent would reign familiar within the journal up until the last writing on November 12th, 1856, which consisted of one sentence written in hardly legible cursive, "I am to die."

Pat finished reading the entirety of the two-hundred-page journal before the spring. There were many distractions while he read it. The senior had been very busy finishing up with school in order to graduate, but still most of his time was spent on jai alai against the barn- even throughout the winter. To a great extent he also helped his grandfather split wood during the winter months, which was more or less a smokescreen to discuss the journal.

Pat told his grandfather one grey January day, "Grandpa Calvin, this whole journal seems unreal."

"I know it's hard to believe all this happened. Amazing how easy it was to declare war! We've killed many innocent people," Grandpa Calvin said.

"But why has this all continued to work Grandpa? Why are we here if we are a war machine nation?"

"Man, you sound like your dad!" Grandpa Calvin said.

It was quite a potent read for a seventeen year old, but Pat would not let it influence his life as his father had. A consciousness arose for the present. A new knowledge developed, leading the teenager to believe a government has the ability to commit malice upon its own citizens and not be held accountable. Along the path of his own journey, though, Pat accepted that whatever happened to himself was a result of his own actions- opposite of his father's victimization ideology. He came to believe that if one needs to blame the government for their grief, maybe they're doing something wrong. First look within before disparaging.

Destiny, nevertheless, would be held within his own hands by the end of senior year. A heightened certainty for his future after high school solidified with graduation approaching in 1980. There became no doubt that a move to Hartford would make the eighteen year old's long-time dream a reality. This move would also somewhat remove the memory of Russell's fall from his mind.

As fate would have it, jai alai had become a professional venue in Sothern New England. Confidence led Pat to believe his skill merited a chance to play professionally in Connecticut. "Gosh, what would Papa Jacques think," came across the young man's mind. By chance, it just so happened that a second cousin on his mother's side lived in Hartford— Jenn Partlow. The moment Pat told his mother his intention to move to Hartford, she thought up the idea that Pat ask Jenny to stay with her. Pat was hesitant at first as he hadn't seen her in ten years. "She would be more than happy to host you," his mother told him.

Pat gathered the courage and called his distant cousin on May 8th, 1980, a week after he turned eighteen and a month before graduation.

"Jenny, how are you? This is your cousin Pat Adams."

"I know. Your mother has already called," Jenn said.

"That's my mom."

"I'm sorry about your dad; she told me everything,"

"No problem. It's actually a type of closure. My brother Mark is the one having problems. He's actually going to move to Boston with a couple of friends at the end of the month."

"It's a tough thing to happen," Jenn said and paused, "So you want to try out for jai alai."

"Yes, that's all I'm good at."

"Pat, it's such a small world. My boyfriend Kenny has some connections to Hartford jai alai, and he already promised me that he would get you a tryout any time you want."

"Are you serious, Jenn? And you won't mind having me stay with you?"

"No problem at all. Your mom told me you need a place to live for a little while."

"Yes, hopefully no longer than a month," Pat said.

"For as long as you want. Family first. When are you going to make the trip?" she asked.

"Mid June, after I graduate."

"Perfect."

The Hartford opportunity seemed to good to be true, but before Pat left he had to keep his word to his mother and graduate. On June 14, 1980, Pat Adams graduated from Pittsfield High School, the first Adams' male to graduate Pittsfield High since Calvin Adams in the twenties. It was the happiest day of Anna's life. But the most difficult part of all was breaking the news to his grandfather.

Only Anna and Grandpa Calvin had attended the school's graduation, which was quite short- it was a class of thirty. Mark had already left for Boston with some friends, in which they brought the remains of Russell's stash—at least what they didn't smoke. Mark thought he would become some huge dealer in the big city holding no interest in Pat's feat.

For Pat there was no graduation party, he didn't want one. Consequently, no one came over after Russell's fall, aside from Mark's friends. Festivities would be shared with his mother and grandfather, who simply took him out for lunch to "The Berkshire Diner". Calvin had no idea about Hartford. The boys didn't feel comfortable talking sports with him. They knew his opinion since an early age. Nonetheless, discussion on Pat's future nearly filled the entirety of the meal at the town diner.

"Grandpa, I'm leaving in a week."

"Where?"

"Hartford."

"What's in Hartford? Who's going to help me now around the farm? You can get into any of these local colleges, you got the grades!"

"I will help," Anna added.

"I'm following my dream. Jai alai is a professional sport there."

"Well, you know what I think of sports," he said. "Our country worries more about a game rather than the poor. The most talented men use their energy for making thousands upon thousands of dollars. They have no interest in improving this world; they just think of themselves. This competitive superior nature is awful. Thinking you're better than someone else pollutes this world."

"Grandpa, I love this sport."

"My dad would be happy," Mother interrupted.

"Well, I know how much time you put into it. I have no control. You achieved something your father or brother could not do. What's to say you will not do very well. I'm just going to miss you around here son. I know we don't talk much, but I've always thought you were a great kid. I love you."

"Thanks, Grandpa. I will never forget what we talked about the day you gave me the journal."

A few other matters were brought up, but Pat's mind was set. He started packing as soon as he arrived home.

The remaining days in Pittsfield were spent practicing.

Chapter Twelve: Hartford

Ever since Russell died, Mark and Pat's relationship died too. Brother felt brother was responsible one way or the other. The two young men would speak no more than a few words to each other each day, even as they shared the same house. Just about a month before graduation, Pat told Mark his plans about Hartford following the phone call with

Jenn. Consequently, the older Adams boy became very jealous.

The discovery that Pat was following his dream suddenly propelled Mark into working on his basketball game again. Every day during the end of May he picked up the basketball from the barn floor. He shot on the net-less hoop for hours. This was the first time seriously practicing since his expulsion. Sadly, his biggest fan's encouragement was silent. Yes, he would play many a stoned pickup games again with his group heading to Boston.

Mark had continued to be a huge basketball fan after his expulsion, he spent many hours idolizing college and pro stars. At the time he learned of Pat's plans, he greatly admired the first Native American All-American from Indiana. The more he watched Barry Word, the Indiana State star, the more he knew he could do the same. Thus, when he heard Pat was materializing his dream into a reality, he thought he could easily do it as well. Not a word was spoke about his intentions when Pat would pass Mark shooting, as Pat had no longer feared the white barn. The choice to move to Boston was partially determined by the Boston Celtics choice to select Barry Word in the draft. More so, however, Boston was the big city.

Like father like son. No conception was held in Mark that ego and drugs were slowly devouring him. The same dependence that destroyed his father was too blocking any chance for achieving his dreams. Yet, Mark still felt he had a chance to miraculously break into the league. Nevertheless, the backup plan in Boston seemed much more realistic- trafficking the remainder of his dad's stash in Boston for income. He thought the substance would pay for his needs, while he prepared to walk onto an NBA team. Mark however held no idea how to earn a tryout, even though he had the talent.

A call was made out to his older brother in Boston June 20th, 1980, the day Pat was leaving for Hartford. The call's purpose was to make Mark aware his younger brother was departing the house. Mark's sole concern during the brief conversation, not thinking of his mother's well-being for an instance, was telling his younger brother that he was dealing in much bigger and better things than their dad ever had.

"I deal with the big boys Pat. I'm doing business with the biggest boss up here!"

Mark, thus, gave up on his dream.

The call drew concern, but when it came to his brother, the past taught Pat, just as it had his mother, that ignorance was bliss. More importantly, Pat was confident that Mark was far away enough that he wouldn't interfere in Hartford. Overwhelming confidence toward the move commenced as soon as Mark left his mind. A confidence he had yet to feel

Another important aspect of the move was that Mark would be far away from his mother in Pittsfield. He was only separated previously for no more than a single evening sleepover. She was nevertheless very supportive. The damaged widow, however, could not handle the horrid reality of another loved one kill himself. Undoubtedly, she would have had a severe breakdown if her oldest stuck around and slowly destroyed himself too.

Pat rationalized jai alai as the only means that led him toward success. He would not let anything get in the way. The departure from any reminder of his father was imperative in addition. Leaving his mother was hard though. Opposite to Mark's quick good-bye, there were many tears accompanying the strong farewell embrace between Anna Adams and her youngest. The passion that grew inside from all of Russell's insults and acts could not be concealed. The unbreakable grip clenched for a minute until Anna released, then Pat. The tear filled mother then spoke.

"I love you son, you will do just fine."

"Thank you. Make sure you get wood from grandpa, he'll take care of you. I love you too," Pat said. He then left in his hand me down green station wagon only packed in the rear.

Chapter Thirteen: Jenny

The trip to Hartford was smooth for a rainy summer feeling day in 1980. Pat arrived at Jenn's two-family house on Fairfield Avenue at five in the evening. The second floor of a large two-family gray house was home. The house, in need of a painting, was located in the South End. The owner John Medonis, lived on the first floor, whom she had contacted about the vacant apartment in 1978. The twenty-three year old, who considered herself to live alone, was able to pay for the large three-bedroom dwelling by waitressing at a popular Hartford night club. The Silver Club also neighbored Hartford Jai Alai within the North Meadows.

Pat opened the unlocked front door that led into the enclosed front hall that presented both the first and second-floor locked front glass wooden doors. He rang the doorbell on the right, which he could tell was for the second floor. The white linen curtain couldn't hide the black stairwell. Ten seconds passed before footsteps were heard running down the stairwell, feet were then seen behind the linen hanging atop the classically designed door.

"Pat," was spoken behind an opening door.

"Jenny." Pat responded in a high-pitched tone toward his eye-catching brunette cousin.

"I haven't seen you in ten years," Jenn said before the two shared a friendly hug.

She was very attractive—a tall brunette, with blue eyes, and a beautiful face.

"I know. It's sure nice of you to share your place with me; you sure you don't mind? I can find a hotel somewhere," Pat said.

"Don't be stupid. It'll be fun. Just park that boat down the hill in the back and come check it out."

She led Pat up the stairs. "Kenny, my boyfriend, will be here in a couple of hours, he pretty much lives here too. I think you two will enjoy each other. Different from where you come from, he will fill you in."

"Sounds good."

The initial appearance was that of cleanliness and emptiness, as she lacked furniture and wall mounts. She first showed Pat to his room. It was a sun-room in the front of the house that had been converted into a bedroom. It had a lot of windows, each bearing a blind that would allow privacy and shade. The only articles of furniture were a single bed and a dresser. Pat set his cesta and all of his bags on the floor next to the oak dresser. Pat then went into the living room to sit on the leather love seat. His seat sat perpendicular to the old worn-in gray couch Jenny sat on.

"Do you want a drink?" she asked.

"I don't think so. I don't want to end up like my dad."

"I'm so sorry about that. He was a good guy, from what I can remember."

"He got out of control." Pat shook his head.

The two talked about her family and his, while she continued to drink for the duration of the night.

"I feel bad. You work hard, and here I am imposing with no money for food or rent. I will look for some construction work, at least until I can get a gig in jai alai," Pat said.

"Don't worry! I make good money, and the owner here, Mr. Medonis, is very kind. He thinks of me as his daughter. I'm telling you just talk to Kenny; he'll get you a gig."

"Nice. So how is Kenny connected to jai alai?"

"Well. You can't tell anyone what I'm going to tell you."

"Sure."

"Kenny's best friend Dan Dellski is the house bookie there."

"Really?" Pat was shocked.

"Yeah, they take bets on games. I guess Kenny makes some good money from Dan's information."

At that instant in Pat's mind appeared the most peculiar thought, 'My father was right this whole time.'

"I don't want to become corrupt," Pat said to Jenn.

"Don't worry. Kenny will take care of you. This is your dream, right?"

If Pat did commit to join in with Kenny and his friend the house bookie, Dan Dellski, Pat knew his involvement would become illegal. He would be a criminal, just as Russell had told him he would. Nevertheless, Pat had never followed his father's words too closely. Anticipation still existed in the eighteen-year-old to see what Kenny had to say.

"Kenny should be here any time now. He's bouncing at the club where I waitress or at least that's what he calls it."

"Oh."

"Yeah," Jenn said, "it took awhile for the two of us to get together, but he's the best thing for me. Yeah we get funny looks, and like Kenny says, 'we're not the norm', but who cares. Why can't we all be colorblind Pat?"

A piece of Jenn's story was missing for Pat's comprehension.

"You sure you don't want a drink, Pat?"

"I shouldn't."

"You know, sadness is contagious. A couple drinks will loosen you up—if you keep everything in, you won't be able to recognize the exterior beauty in life or people. Pat, you'll grow ugly inside. As you hide yourself, your dreams will be forbidden from you. The only solution to overcome sadness is to let it out! A drink may help."

"OK, I'll have one beer."

She immediately rose, headed toward the fridge, and grabbed a beer. While she was away, Pat heard the door open downstairs. Kenny had arrived. Strong heavy steps approached as Pat sat on the living room couch that neighbored the doorway from the stairs.

Kenneth Carter was nothing like Pat expected, even as he already knew Kenny as a corrupt man. The moment Pat looked over at the body that entered, he fully open his eyes and extended his neck upward.

In walked a black man, who stood six foot seven, and weighed near two hundred seventy pounds.

"Is this Pat, Jenny?" Kenny smiled with his pointed jaw and a fresh high fade.

"Sure is," she answered after handing Pat his beer.

"Nice to meet you, Kenny." Pat put down his beer, stood up, and shook Kenny's hand. He felt very small.

"Pleasure, Pat."

Instantly, Pat could sense Kenny had a kind, welcoming disposition.

"So you hope to make a jai alai team I hear?" Kenny asked.

"Yes. I have been working very hard."

The large man then took Pat by surprise. "Let's see what you got."

"What?"

"Out back. Jenn's built-in garage foundation is concrete. She has great lighting out there. Just don't break a first floor window!"

"You won't have to worry about that." Pat smiled.

At ten o'clock at night, Pat grabbed the sticks from the sun-room and accompanied Kenny down the back stairs. Kenny hit the light switch right as the two walked out the back screen door of the basement. Déjà vu arose for Pat as Kenny housed his hoop on the wall Pat was to serve on. Side by side they stood fifteen feet away from the garage with lights that caused mild squinting. Pat then decided to move his car to make sure it wouldn't obstruct his performance.

As Pat held the cesta and ball, right before he was going to show his skill, Kenny explained the circumstances. "My white boy best friend growing up is mixed up in this whole jai alai thing, but he makes a whole lot of money as a bookie. If you know how to play, Ski can make this work."

"I was taught by a very talented man!" Pat said.

"Then there should be no issue. Let it rip."

It took about ten total volleys for Kenny to tell Pat to stop. "I'll call Dan tomorrow. You will be big news- an American white boy who can play. I don't think one American plays here in Hartford. You fell into the right place."

"Yeah, it's a small world."

In returning back upstairs, Pat had the second entire beer of his life with Kenny.

Subsequent to the sound of cracking one, Kenny said, "You know I was a big-time athlete. I had a full D-1 scholarship. I actually made the Knicks roster. Yep I made the big show."

"Serious, that's amazing. What college?" Pat asked.

"University of West Hartford—but you know what, Pat? It isn't the sports I love most. It's our history. Do I look like someone that can recite every president."

"Really."

"The past presents the future," Kenny said.

"I agree. So did my dad. You know what Kenny, come to think of it, I have something I brought along you may cherish."

"What's that?" Kenny asked as he sat at the edge of the couch.

"A journal."

"What kind of journal?"

"One written by my ancestor after his time in the War of 1812."

"Are you serious? Get out of here. That is the most fascinating of times."

"Hold on, I'll go get it." Pat fetched it and returned. "Here."

"Holy shit! This is what I spent the majority of my junior year researching. Do you know about The Hartford Convention?"

"No clue," Pat said.

Kenny instantaneously opened the heirloom. Henri's work was read through for about five minutes.

"What you have in here is the War of Detroit, it is the start of the war. What I know most of is the end of the war though. The war ended because of a convention that happened here in Hartford. It was this Hartford Convention that disrupted a war based on false pretense. The convention was purely manifested because of the New England politicians aligned with virtue and constitutional law. Inexplicably, no one has any clue of this affair."

"I never heard of it."

"Let's get some drinks at my work, we gotta talk. I'll give you a little tour of Hartford. This is where my roots are. You have a lot to learn country boy."

The second Pat shut the door of the Cadillac parked in front of the house, he took a glance in the back seat. Nearly a hundred books and memoirs formed a literary mountain. There was no doubt for Pat that Kenny had memorized all the material in each one of those books.

Kenny then pushed down the pedal. They sped around Hartford for a half hour. Kenny showed Pat the north, south, and west end. "There's Kennelly School, where I went to elementary school." Many landmarks were also seen, as well as the college Kenny attended. The destination of the tour was finally reached as they arrived at the Silver Club around midnight.

The two opened their doors after Kenny parked in the third closest reserved parking spot. They got out and headed toward the foreboding club. Following about ten steps Pat paused. He realized they were in the heart of the industrial sector of Hartford. With one glance it became obvious, the neighboring building read "Hartford Jai Alai" in large green letters. The dream now stood a hundred feet away. Not a thought of corruption arose though. With another twenty steps, Pat stopped again, striking up a stare right before he entered the late-night club. The dream was reaching fruition.

The entrance for the night club was surrounded with bright silver Christmas lights and a large neon sign above the door that read "Silver." Flashlights then blinded Pat with the entrance in sight. Bouncers dressed in all black, who seemed urgent to talk with Kenny, greeted the large black man at the door. He, however, brushed them aside and simply told them, "Later."

Inside, Kenny knew everyone. All the old timers nodded as he passed. He had now worked at the Silver Club for a few years. His personality, product, or appearance had touched every single patrons mind differently. Pat was no exception.

Inside the dim lit club, not only did the employees flock toward Kenny, but nearly all the patrons sought his attention. The owner was first to come over. The clean-cut sharp dressed boss shook Kenny's hand and then introduced himself to Pat.

"Mike Dibella, nice to meet you."

"Mike, this guy knows how to play your game, boss man," Kenny said.

"Really! Make sure Ski meets up with him soon."

The owner Dibella then looked at Pat and spoke in a calm manner, "Relax, make yourself at home, drink as much as you want on the house." He then left to entertain another table.

"What a place. You're a popular guy," Pat told Kenny.

"I do a lot of business with these people. You want another beer?"

"Sure."

Kenny got a couple of drinks at the bar, had a quick conversation with the bartender, and then sat back down on a stool at the tall slim round table across from Pat. All his attention was given to Pat. It quickly became obvious why he did not pay mind to everyone else. After a gulp, he continued on with talk of the war, which Kenny had a lot to say. Besides his professors, he never before encountered anyone who knew about The War of 1812, or who would listen to him on the matter.

"The war altogether was a bunch of BS, Pat! The true motives of the war were to acquire the outlet of the St. Lawrence, rob the Indians of their land, erect a standing army, and to increase the power and patronage of the president."[xix]

Kenny was overwhelmingly energized for this subject. "Just think about what slave-owning Jefferson said, 'the tree of liberty must be refreshed from time to time with the blood of patriots and tyrants. It is its natural manure.'"

"You see, Pat, some Federalists and Democratic-Republicans alike, all held the vehemence that they were the sole proprietors of the natural landscape. Yes, our founders claimed ownership of the vast wilderness and held the power to transform it into whatever they desired! Not to mention, enslaving men who simply held a different complexion, all in order to stockpile riches."

"Pat, in my historical account, there existed a disparity in opinion for the best interest of this country- near the beginning of the nineteenth century. Thank the heavens, there were men who had held civic virtues. But, the Jefferson Democracy amassed too much power. Thus, there was no denying the system dependent on amassing money. This capitalistic covetousness still runs our policies today. We were fixed on making limitless money, not balancing things in existence."

"Back then the precedent was set in which noble conscious acts would go unheeded by the very men who sat on their bags of gold. Insanity for riches and popularity, even if obtained by ill measures, denied the very literature, art, philosophy, and civic virtue, which great societies are built upon."

"Those for expansion by any means stood against those who governed to improve what presently existed. There is no doubt the civil war had its seeds planted in 1812. Even before 1812, 'the disaffection of the federalists was publicly expressed by Josiah Quincy, of Massachusetts, in a speech in 1811 on the admission of Louisiana: 'if this bill passes,' he said, 'it is my deliberate opinion that it is virtually a dissolution of this Union; that it will free the States from their moral obligation; and, as it will be the right of all, so it will be the duty of some, definitely to prepare for a separation, amicably if they can, violently if they must.'"

"'Hence, with the embargo and then the war in 1812, portions of our government were the most eager and successful, in their efforts to ruin [New England].'[xx] 'As Britain was admitted, generously and nobly admitted to be the soul of the confederacy, and as Mr. Madison knew this as well as we did; he affirmed in his message, that the success of the British arms was favorable to our commerce [and] was friendly to the independence and tranquility of all the world.'"[xxi]

"See Pat, as the army moved toward Canada in 1812, pre-existing America was defenseless- the Atlantic coast especially. As Madison had declared war and sent the army to invade, state residents, consequently, were thus being called into the militia by their federal government- a measure which was justified as a means for defense, but truly the intent was purely to use those men for invasion. States were also becoming broke, as they too had to support their own defense. The extended state militia would be the sole defense for the New England coastal towns attacked by the British maritime power. It was an obvious calculation that New England states were to 'retain a reasonable portion of the taxes collected within the said States' and also for 'State armies to be held in readiness to serve for the defense of the New England States upon the request of the governor of the State invaded.'[xxii]"

"According to the constitution at the time of an invasion, the militia was to be formed by the state, and then trained and led by the government. However, some states refused to share their own militia in 1812. 'The Governor of Connecticut refused to send militia, declaring that he must yield to obedience to the paramount authority of the Constitution and laws.'[xxiii] As the war advanced and the territory of Massachusetts in the district of Maine was invaded by British troops an urgent call for protection was made upon the general government; but even in the crisis Massachusetts would not permit her militia to pass under the control of national military officers'.[xxiv] These independent stands taken by the New England governments disrupted a standard so dangerous to the liberties of the country."

Kenny continued to keep his intensity throughout his history lesson. Pat was actually thoroughly entertained. But his mind was wandering on what neighboring Hartford Jai Alai was like inside. He could see the large building through the tinted glass. Nevertheless, Kenny kept both the facts and drinks rolling in front of Pat.

"Even before 1812 Pat, the militia's role in the revolution was for 'members to furnish their own weapons, form companies according to neighborhoods, choose officers by ballot of the men, and convene a general military council of representatives from each company. Civic virtue, rather than compulsion, would serve as the basis for the actions of all involved.'[xxv]"

"The federal government could summon the militia to active duty to enforce the laws of the United States, suppress insurrection, or repel invasion, but no militiaman could be required to serve the United States for more than three months in any one year.[xxvi]"

"The militia would not be treated accordingly, though. The political majority clearly did not hold Federalist principles. Federalists would greatly diminish with the southern slave vote and the admission of the large territory of Louisiana. Sadly it was those certain men of the Federalist Party who never 'studied the art of tickling the people, for they had been too intent upon doing them good, to think of that. The democratic leaders had studied to give them good words, and served them with bad fare. They had talked everything well; they had done everything ill. They are good talkers, but poor workmen: they had much fancy, but little judgment; they had the appearance of great zeal, but they had no wisdom.'[xxvii]

"The time came when it was an absolute necessity for New England to act. Sadly The Hartford Convention, which disclosed such important remedies for our troubled nation, also marked the end of the Federalist Party. It was altogether a sinister sign of the times. Expansionist politicians manipulated the Hartford Convention to appear as an anti-American convention. On the contrary, the convention at no time performed a manifestation against the government. Rather, it served as the most potent peaceful disobedience toward political corruption.

"The entire convention was recorded and performed with the utmost respect for the prosperity of the country, which would not have even been necessary if we simply avoided the great conflict altogether. 'Even the subject of impressment, for the purpose of getting rid of which it had been exclusively maintained, almost from the beginning, had been formally abandoned, and the controversy had in October, 1814, in fact, though secretly, assumed its true character, which was that of a war for the support of the personal popularity of the national administration, and not for the protection of the rights and honor of the nation.'[xxviii] In forming a peace treaty including a security against impressment, the justification for the declaration of war against England, was abandoned."

Kenny paused, took a deep breath, and continued. "Pat, you get what I'm saying. Let me put it simply. 'Mr. Madison said in 1795 wars produce armies, debts and taxes; armies, debts and taxes are the known instruments by which the many are brought under the domination of the few.'[xxix] 'Had not the New England States made a firm stand in defense of their constitutional privileges and prerogatives, the next war in which the nation were to be entangled with would have reduced the individual states power, placing them at the mercy of the national government. Little would have been necessary to declare a war- whether true or false. [A simple manipulation that] the country was in danger of invasion [would spawn] a demand for any number of the militia that the executive might think proper to order, to be placed under the command of United States officers, and made liable to be marched to any rendezvous that the president, or any subordinate officer under him, should direct. This would at a stroke deprive the states of their militia—their only safeguard against tyranny and oppression—and the national government would at once be in possession of a power sufficient to overthrow their liberties and independence.'[xxx]"

"It's getting late. I talked your ear off. I have just one more point. These men in New England were great men. 'Remember, that although one set of men [tried] to drive down, from the high elevation of prosperity it had reached under other; remember, that the mad rulers, who seemed bent on destroying everything that was left; were not immortal; remember too, that although an honest, patriotic, and intelligent people were deluded, and that although even when the delusion was dissipate, even when they began to see, and to see clearly too, with the eyes of their own understandings, they delayed the acknowledgement of their convictions, yet no people ever had, or ever can have, a motive powerful enough; to make them the voluntary victims of unmerited and unnecessary sufferings; of self inflicted, but unavailing torture.'[xxxi]"

Silence ensued for a couple minutes.

"I hope I didn't embarrass myself." Kenny chuckled.

"No, all this confirms what Henri wrote."

Consequent to all the drinks handed to Pat, this was the first time he felt drunk. And he liked it a lot. Listening to Kenny brag in a nightclub about what he knew only expanded Pat's dream. Glances over his shoulder to the neighboring building were a constant. It was a great first night in Hartford, but Pat knew when he woke up it was time to get a tryout. The night was not just done with leaving the club. Kenny had a lot to say on the ride home.

Chapter Fourteen: Kenneth Carter

"You like that club?" Kenny started up his Cadillac.

"Yes, I had a lot of fun."

"You know how I make money there?"

"You're a bouncer," Pat said.

"Don't listen to your cousin; she's a sugar-coater. I sell drugs there."

He reached over to his glove box and opened it. "See all these bags?"

"Yes," Pat quietly replied as he noticed a gun too.

"That's five grand right there! Are you surprised. You didn't think an educated black man would deal in this huh. I've been exposed to this my whole life man. In college it was all around man, but I never dabbled in the beginning. I just wanted to learn and learn and learn. The only reason I played ball was cause of Ski."

"Education to me, Pat, is a plain joke. I am lucky I loved educating myself, but I don't do shit with it. I tell ya, I've seen a lot of potential go wasted here in the heart beat. Hartford is a sad place. No doubt, failure starts with the family and then continues into school. For a strong society, strong families must exist. That ain't the case here man. With the lack of consistency at home, there is no consistency in the schools. Dire consequences my friend."

"Ha, when I was in Elementary School at Kennelly they had something called 'No one shall fail.' Whoever's bright idea it was held no model for the over achievers. These kids were bored stupid, myself included. If you asked me to fix the education system here, I'd start with adding a gifted and talented program. Instead of turning everyone into robots- making everyone equal and dumming down kids- I would promote their interest. Rather than use the reading and math specialists to even out the back with the front, I'd use the most intelligent to work with the most intelligent. Here in this society I'd want the genius to go off on his own and learn as much as humanly possible. 'Go figure it out boy.'

"And I sure have figured it out! My best means of income is slinging dope. I make all this money through clientele. I don't do any labor; why you think I'm so fat. Customers first call me at the club to set up a buy. When they get to the doorman, who already knows what is owed, they hand over the money. I then get the call inside. We meet at the last bathroom stall where I hand over the goods. It has been flawless so far. Keep your mouth shut, things will work out great for you too."

"No problem," Pat said.

"Man I knew right away I could trust you Pat, you are one cool white boy!"

All this was so confusing for Pat. This incredibly articulate black man was also a brilliant drug dealer. It was hard to believe that his cousin was dating this polarizing man.

Jenny had first met Kenny at the Silver Club where they had worked together with little contact for the first few months. He pursued her for a while to no avail. She had never dated a black man. One night she had a change of heart after a difficult night of bickering with the bar staff. She finally gave in to go out on a date. Soon thereafter she became very happy with him. "I won't do you no wrong girl."

With the remaining drive being silent, subsequent to the discovery of Kenny's means of income, the two arrived on Fairfield Avenue. They walked in, shared a 'good night', and went to their rooms. The next day, the moment Kenny left for work, Pat told his cousin everything the two did in Hartford the previous night.

Jenn responded, "Yeah, Kenny is an interesting guy. At first we were mocked everywhere. I was so uncomfortable going out with him. But through time we have come to accept ignorance."

Kenny's story followed.

Kenny was born and raised in Hartford, but it was a white family who took in the youth after his drug addicted parents had died in a fire. The lifestyle change, however unfortunate it had initially seemed, proved to be rather beneficial for Kenny. Rules and provisions were accommodated that served all the means necessary to develop a potential that ultimately landed him in college-where he excelled not only in the classroom but also on the court.

Following the death of his parents, he was still young enough in fifth grade to become academically aware. Strict rules were to be implemented on the black youth the moment he moved in with a neighborhood Polish family, the Dellski's. The new conditions were the bridge to friendship with the future jai alai bookie, Dan Dellski- otherwise "Ski". High expectations for school and behavior were implemented daily by mother and father upon Kenny as they were for Dan.

Subsequent to consistent discipline, Kenny was offered a basketball and academic scholarship during the final year of high school. He became so good at the Division I level that the Knicks, in the second round with the thirty-fifth pick, drafted Kenny Carter in 1978. Moreover, he earned a political science degree, tools he never used until he enlightened Pat. Sadly, drugs and a gambling debt put an end to his temporary superstar lifestyle- yet he somehow always kept his spirits high.

The second night in Hartford was nowhere near as enthralling as the first night. It wasn't until late that excitement would ensue for the teenager. Anticipation was felt all day by Pat in regard to Kenny mentioning a jai alai tryout.

Kenny left the house at 10:00 a.m. to supply some early users, not to return until 1:00 a.m. Jenn had the evening off, but was in bed near ten p.m. after joining Pat for some television. When Kenny arrived home from work, Pat was watching *Late Night*. He couldn't sleep. Pat could tell Kenny was partying hard with his arrival. Kenny stimulated Pat the moment he walked in.

"I got you a tryout tomorrow."

"Great! Wow! You're a man of your word, Kenny."

"Ski said to come around two in the afternoon."

"Seriously, thanks so much, Kenny."

"Just be careful Pat. I dug a big ditch for myself a few years back. Before I got drafted, I messed a lot of things up for myself senior year. I decided to join Ski's gambling ring. I was so young and dumb. My professional career was tarnished the moment I flawed a game in college. To think poorly performing for my own benefit would truly benefit myself," Kenny said.

"Really? Jenn told me a little about the Dellskis raising you, but I didn't realize what else you got into." Pat was very intrigued.

"Everything I'm gonna tell you is the straight-up truth. I've been through some crazy shit!"

Kenny then told Pat his whole side of the story. The theme of corruption drew familiarity for Pat his first two evenings with Kenny. Dan Dellski, Kenny's best friend since youth, was no exception. Dan was the vehicle that led Kenny toward corruption. Accompanying Kenny's departure for freshman year of college, Ski became a potent underworld player . He knew everything about everyone involved with gambling or drugs in Hartford County.

Ski was not always on the wrong side, though. He had known Kenny since elementary school and Kenny truly knew what was deep inside of his friend.

Kenny lived a couple of houses over from the Dellski's before the fire. Awoken by flames in his room, Kenny jumped out his first-floor bedroom window and ran to Dan's house for safety. The same bus route first initiated the friendship, which led the black youth to find comfort in a white house. Dan too was in the same class as Kenny.

The two were opposites—Kenny was tall and lean, Dan was short and fat; Kenny could dunk, Dan could jump four inches. But the Dellski's were quite charitable. The middle class happily married couple offered to house Kenny until family could be notified. Who, come to find out, would all refuse. However different the two, an immeasurable friendship spawned directly when the two practiced basketball the night following the death of Kenny's parents. Little was said as Kenny shot near five hundred shots while Dan rebounded and passed back. It was that same night that Kenny first branded the nickname Ski upon Dan. Tradition was born. Henceforth, they played ball every day- rain or shine.

Kenny held the conviction that he owed his basketball ability to Ski. Dan was the only one who pressured the six-foot-two inch fifteen-year-old to practice every day. Ski would always tell Kenny, "You're going to be great. Just practice your free-throws some more."

Ski actually loved sports more than Kenny, basketball especially. Dan adored the game; he knew everything about every NBA player—points per game, rebounds per game, college attended. There was one problem—Ski was short, heavy, and most importantly, not an athlete. Hence, he lived vicariously through Kenny. Nothing would have made him happier than to see his massive best friend live up to his potential.

Through the hard work the two put in together, Kenny received a full scholarship as a result of his stellar career at Hartford High. Kenny would only have to travel a short distance for college. He left the south end for the West End. The little known division one University of West Hartford would grow regional acclaim through Kenny's athletic ability.

College required Kenny to leave his adopted home and best friend. Kenny did not mind. He was very excited. Taken in by a new family had given Kenny the ability to adapt to most situations. Dan, on the other hand, would quickly lose the friend that consumed all his time. Soon thereafter, Ski began to participate in sports in a far different manner. He held so much knowledge in college and professional sports that he began to use that information to make some quick money at first. Researching lines satisfied the everyday void Kenny had filled, but Dan still visited Kenny weekly during the first three years of college. And he never missed a home game.

During this period, Dan Dellski became known as Ski throughout the streets of Hartford. To Ski, there were no other options—the only reason he enjoyed high school was because of Kenny. Academics were not his strength either. He only graduated because of the help he received on his homework nearly every day from Kenny. Grades didn't matter much; he was too busy formulating player stats' sitting at the desk. Popularity also materialized because of his relationship with the star athlete. He was flocked by all the other students at high school games. Ski sure rode the attention all the way until graduation. Come college, relationships Kenny's stature connected for Ski, were of a much more lucrative nature. Nevertheless, Ski discovered his gambling ability after high school, which won over 75 percent of the time. He was very good at betting.

Ever since he was a boy there was a supernatural psychic intuition inside Ski. No one else ever knew this but Kenny. Especially for sports, Ski had the ability to coincidently discover the major factors that would determine the outcome.

Coincidently, with Kenny's departure to college, Ski was able to meet up with a friend of his dad's, Billy, who was a petty bookie. Billy was the first to open the gates to Ski. The teen soon acquired customers who needed a variety of fixes. Helpless drug addicts to gamblers looking for free scratch tickets came to Ski. Whatever was hanging outside the Maple Ave. Corner Store was an easy target for the rookie bookie.

In terms of drugs, Ski befriended a drug dealer at Al's Sports Bar one January evening while watching Kenny play a road game at Buffalo his freshman year. The dealer lost a quick bet, but soon evened it out. Ski quickly discovered there was a much larger market for drugs than for gambling in Hartford. A deal was made that allowed Ski to barter with the dealer dirt cheap drugs for his outstanding gambling debts. In turn, the drugs exponentially grew into a two-hundred percent profit. However many drugs Dan Dellski attained he never took any. He just began supplying them for profit.

The streets soon were buzzing with the name Ski. From the peddlers on corners, the drunks anchored in the sports bar or those at Uncle Al's Gentlemen's Club, they all knew the name. He quickly got his name out to nearly all of Hartford, gamblers and addicts alike. Exponential growth grew. The potency of the products he distributed were intense and never cut or pinched into, clients were thrilled. In terms of gambling, he seemed to always be omnipresent in order for an addict to make a game time bet. Building his reputation,

Ski still continued to hang out with Kenny in the dorms, at college parties, and in college bars.

Most importantly, it was the games that Ski loved.

Drug dealing or gambling, however, were not discussed between the two friends at first, as Kenny's energy was entirely directed toward basketball and his political science courses.

Sophomore year, however, an argument finally arose when a transaction manifested itself in Kenny's dorm room for one of his teammates. Ski told all of Kenny's teammates to keep the dealings out of his sight. Nonetheless, there was one player who couldn't control himself and hunted Ski down in the dorm room. Kenny too was present. The final agreement to the argument was that Kenny didn't want Ski to bring his stuff around the dorm room. The intelligent big man knew many consequences would come if caught. Kenny could get kicked out of school, or even worse end up as his parents.

It was inevitable that Kenny would discover Ski's undertaking at some point though. He had begun supplying drugs to half the dorm's residents through interaction at parties, all without Kenny's knowledge freshman year. Discovery of the gamblers and addicts within the University of West Hartford was quite easy.

The rule continued for a couple more years, Kenny's talent was rising through the Civic Center's roof. Senior year was much different. Ski and Kenny moved in together Kenny's final year of eligibility. The college athlete had no money, but he wanted to live off campus as all the other seniors had. Outside funds did not exist. Kenny was cut off at eighteen from the Dellski's. The only way possible would be through Ski's assistance, who assured him he could easily take care of it—Ski was rolling in the dough. Without delay, great temptations were presented the very first night the two stayed over in their small two-bedroom condo about a month outside of preseason conditioning. The dorm room rules no longer applied.

"If I pay, drugs stay!" Ski told Kenny.

Ski had a couple clients over for a football game their first night in on a Friday. As Kenny sat in the room, Ski was handed a hundred dollar bill by their guests, in which he responded by handing over a good sized bag of amphetamines.

Ski and his guests next celebrated a "Cheers!" for the transaction, followed with the guzzling of beers. Kenny would slowly drink a few as well. The promising star greatly enjoyed both the game and the jovial guests.

In years previous, Ski kept his transactions out of Kenny's sight pretty well. Ski would attend college parties with the various dorm roommates Kenny was assigned each year, while the basketball star, on the other hand, spent his weekend nights reading and researching his own curiosities at the campus library. However, the moment they lived back together, along with the return of all students from summer break at the end of August 1977, it became clear for Kenny as to how many of his peers used Ski's services at all hours of the day. A professor even stopped by. Acquaintances could not be denied by Kenny, as there were many attractive ladies who stopped by the condo and used Ski's services as well. Partying thus took precedence that fall.

Kenny's new habits were a far cry from the blood, sweat and tears that made him first team All-Northeastern Conference his junior season. He began his senior year with All-American expectations. In previous seasons, his work ethic was incomparable to any teammate—staying after every practice for free-throws, jumping rope for ten minutes every morning, or doing suicides for a half hour. There is no doubt the 'work for everything' philosophy was instilled when the two lived in the Dellski home. However, the two did not train once Kenny left for college. Ski's dedication to gambling and drug dealing would take over for his dedication to Kenny's basketball career. Under Ski's roof, Kenny too would begin to dedicate his effort in the wrong direction.

Chapter Fifteen: The Gamble

By senior season, Ski was acquiring large amounts of drugs from his gambling commission, which was of a much greater monetary value than when he first started. He disclosed this formula to Kenny their first night in the condo. It quickly became obvious that nearly all Kenny's teammates and prior roommates used one or another of Ski's services. Curiosity as to what he was missing set in. The most familiar faces on campus were coming over all throughout the day, staying for hours upon a time with Kenny and Ski- always offering a bump.

In deep, Ski kept his principles. He never got careless and used his product. Ultimately, he would control the drugs and spreads within the college by Kenny's senior year, along with constant outside clientele. And, sure enough, in his final year, Kenny too wanted in, and not only with drugs.

It was a great setup- the friends were able to live together again during Kenny's senior year in a furnished condo. Kenny made out great, as Ski paid the rent. He was on top of the college world. The basketball star was also able to entertain all the offers from the clients inside the condo who were looking for someone to join them while they marred their spirit.

Soon word spread around campus that both the star athlete and the great drug connection could be found under the same roof. Weeks before the regular season tipoff maximum capacity parties would ensue inside the condo nearly every Thursday through Saturday night. Women, the gang of Ski's customers, college and non-college clientele, all formed the steady flow in the cramped condo.

Kenny did not mind who came in and out of the apartment. He was flying high everyday. Ski was using the incredible earnings to pay for everything. Kenny did, however, need more money to take out the long line of women who were showing him great affection. There was Kim a Caucasian brunette from Stamford; Jessie a beautiful black girl who was a freshman from New Jersey; Elizabeth was a blonde from Cleveland.

During the quiet spells, complaints arose as to how Kenny had no money. One night a few days before the first game of the season Ski told Kenny, "I've been thinking about something for a while now."

A discussion broke out that would change everything. The theme was based on what Kenny thought the outcome in the opening game of his senior season would be. He told Ski that West Hartford would beat Central Connecticut by more than the twelve-point spread.

For the first time, Kenny Carter would use Ski's services. He put money Ski lent him on a game he played in. He was very confident on the outcome. In Kenny's estimation he had no other way to obtain money now that basketball was going to take up all his time. The realization set in on how much money he needed to maintain the clothes, booze, and women he had become accustomed to. He figured the hundred-dollar bet with his best friend, the college bookie, was easy money. Moreover, Ski was ecstatic at the implications. Accordingly, he would bet the most ever. A thousand dollars would be bet on Kenny's certainty.

Sure enough, West Hartford easily won by twenty-two. Ski sat courtside. Kenny only missed three shots all game. Kenny Carter would make the front page of the *Hartford Courant* sports section, which read "Kenny's Court," as he had scored thirty points and grabbed ten rebounds.

This first attempt was so successful and easy that Kenny and Ski both craved more. Success would thereafter come easier each game for a short span. Nearly every game was fixed by Kenny's effort. Thousands were won. Money so easy that Kenny would perform poorly to lose games against difficult rivals- all in order to earn a couple thousand dollars extra.

As the money poured in, Kenny continued to party, purchasing amphetamines every day from Ski, who didn't think anything of it. The consequences of such choices, nevertheless, would quickly impact his academics gravely. Luckily for Kenny, he salvaged his degree only because of the three-point-four grade point average he brought into his one-three GPA senior year.

One constant, nonetheless, were Ski's attendance of home games. He never missed one. Every home game was at the extravagant Hartford Civic Center, where everyone dressed their finest. During poor performances, he was at times, the only West Hartford fan in attendance with a smile.

Kenny's first fixed poor performance came against UConn. He was not confident against the stronger team. The game was determined from the outset, in which he missed four lay-ups in the first five minutes. He had many opportunities for easy baskets, but he purposefully spoiled nearly all of them. It was a game West Hartford could have won. However, Kenny made sure they would lose by at least seven, as the spread was six. At the time, he did not realize his performance hindered his once-promising high draft position.

Kenny's once-positively-motivated best friend was now solely motivated by money rather than the love for a game. Ski shifted support toward the drug dealing and gambling Kenny positively influenced living together. He was more than happy when Kenny purchased a twenty sac. Rather than support a great performance, Ski was most pleased by missed lay-ups during an unfavorable match-up. In addition for Kenny, a great dependency for substance was in full motion during this span. He felt the drugs made him a superior athlete.

In recalling the times to Pat, Kenny said, "We both became so blind, we forgot about the hard work that brought us to the position we had earned. What fools we were to think we could stop working hard."

There happened to be one very positive aspect Ski learned fast through winning so much money so easily- the more you take, the more will be wanted back. In Ski's case this was especially true, because he worked inside the underworld. On their third bet together, Ski made an eight-thousand-dollar bet on the UConn game for himself, while he also made Kenny a two-thousand-dollar bet.

No one had ever made such large bets on the University of West Hartford's regular season games with Billy the Breaker, Ski's only bookie.

Billy held a dark appearance—pale, bald, always in black, shades on constantly, missing a few teeth. He always wore the same black jean jacket with black jeans. Scruff covered his face, but never a beard, and he always smelled of cigarettes. Billy worked with Ski's father at Colt Firearms, where the two shared an amicable relationship. Billy came over the Dellski house often to watch sports and have some beers.

Ski's early business ventures first began one night Billy came over to watch a basketball game. No sooner than Billy sat down, had he discovered the recent high school graduate's sports intuition. The moment Ski's dad went to get a beer; Billy told the teenager that he could make a lot of money through sports, "A bet can be placed on any game you want through me."

Billy saw how passionate Ski was toward sports, but in all honestly, he felt he could use Ski to make him a lot of money. One thing about Billy was he had a very small clientele- only family or easy money. Billy told Pat his only rule their first bet, "You tell no one my name!"

A couple bets a week came about for the first couple weeks, but once Pat hit the college scene the young man made gold. Billy got 10% on all bets Pat won, except the bets Pat placed for himself. This was seized upon once Kenny started playing in college games. Ski knew which games Kenny's team would win and what games they would lose. Bets made the game more exciting. Ski made his first bet at the age of eighteen. And within a four-year span, their relationship produced thousands of bets and dollars for Ski per week. Every bet was made through Billy the Breaker. Surprisingly, most losses came from the University of West Hartford games before the scheme.

Billy, personally, was no big-time bookie, even while holding such an intimidating name, but he was connected to the underworld through family. The Breaker was the provided nickname all because Billy was known for breaking his nephew's kneecap due to the attempt to change a bet he made during the first quarter of Super Bowl XIII, in which the nephew would not pay what he owed on the initial bet.

Billy made clear that he had the ability to make any bet for Ski until an hour before a game. Henceforth, it did not take Ski long to become his most successful subordinate-spotting games moments before tipoff.

Trouble, nonetheless, would arise with the success Ski received through West Hartford Basketball in '77. He bet more with every new game. At least, he lost here and there during the previous three years. The close games were his favorite, two or three point spread; he lost those often.

Billy consequently would confront him for the first time during the payment for the UConn win. All the earnings Ski won from betting on the University of West Hartford had eliminated any profit for Billy's uncle, Mike Dibella, or himself. "This guys never lost this season Billy."

Billy confronted Ski at the sports bar where he did most of his business with those clients not attending the college. The Breaker told Ski, "I can't take bets with you any longer."

"Thank you for all the business kid, but I'm done placing your bets."

Billy handed over the ten thousand Billy's uncle owed Ski and Kenny. Dibella was not happy. He had lost a substantial amount of money on games no one else was betting on.

Billy then told Ski, "No hard feelings, but this is out of my league."

The Silver Club's business card was handed over to conclude the meeting. "Get a hold of my uncle Mike Dibella here. Now you have to go through the source if you want to keep going. Make sure you call him the Boss."

Chapter Sixteen: The Boss

It was a no brainer to contact the Boss. Ski needed to be connected to someone with principal and high esteem throughout the underworld. The young man wanted to be respected by all. He was winning some major bets. The decision was made to visit Billy's uncle at the address given the following day, as Kenny had a game that evening.

Michael "The Boss" Dibella owned the brand new Silver Club, which was becoming the hot spot in the center of industrial Hartford. Nearly every worker within a mile radius would come for at least one cocktail after a full day of labor, while taking pleasure in the attractive waitresses. Ski chose to visit the alluring club to set up the next West Hartford game alone.

About four in the afternoon, Ski stepped one foot through the open glass door into the dim club when a bouncer stopped him. Ski told the bouncer that Billy sent him to see the Boss. The bouncer then pointed to an older gray-white haired man dressed in an entire light blue suit wearing sunglasses. Holding no fear, in doing business with Billy for four years, the twenty-one-year-old walked up to the Boss and told him, "Boss, I want to make a bet."

The aged sharp dressed man simply said, "Call me Mike."

Ski got right down to business. "Mike, I would like to make a wager on the next University of West Hartford home game against the University of Buffalo."

"So you are the one making all this money. What's your name, kid?"

"They call me Ski. Yeah, they're a good team. My buddy plays for them. This time I want to bet ten thousand on Buffalo."

"I heard around of you." The boss then simply replied with a grin and a nod. He then clearly wrote Ski, the wager, and the line. The page in the note pad was set. "You're betting against your buddy, huh?"

"Buffalo's good."

This time Ski was going to take Buffalo with the three points. Kenny was not confident against his solid upstate New York rival. The decision was made, again he was going to have an off night.

"Good Luck," the boss said as Ski departed out of the club.

Game time! Not only did Kenny not make a shot, but the potential All-American fouled out in the first half as the team was trailing by twenty points. Kenny walked toward the bench and the only thought he held behind the sulking face was that they just won ten thousand dollars.

Never had the idea that unwanted attention was brought upon himself and Ski with the twenty-five-point Buffalo win. They thought they were invincible.

Ski visited the Silver Club the following day just past happy hour to collect. The club was quiet during the lull. However, Ski would soon feel great excitement. Not only did the twenty-one-year-old have a gun immediately pointed to his temple at the bar by the same bouncer that originally greeted him at the entrance. But this time he was then transferred to Dibella, also holding a gun, who wedged it into the young man's rib cage. Ski was then forced downstairs into the dark basement. "I'm going to be killed," raced through Ski's head.

The boss quickly interrogated the scared, rising bookie the second he sat on the lone stool in the middle of the single light bulb lit room. The gun would stay on his temple as he sat. With the one bulb hanging from the ceiling above Ski, the boss asked, "How have you easily won over twenty-five-thousand dollars of mine without losing once!"

The boss then shouted, "What do you know?"

With his life in the hands of the boss, Ski instantly gave up the entire scam—every single fixed game was disclosed. Kenny's poor play was described completely. Tears rolled down his cheeks as the anxiety of uncertainty forced trembling. Dibella paused for a minute, removing the gun while Ski buried his face inside his hands. The boss absorbed the whole scenario. All he wanted was to be in on the next game.

"Prove this to me."

Ski had no problem sharing the scheme. The boss next came over and patted the deflated kid on the back. Swiftly, with a reach into the boss's pocket, Ski was then handed the bundle of money that was owed the sobbing twenty-one-year-old. Ski never had a gun to his head before, and this incident brought about a change. Subsequently, he truly became "Ski," as he learned to never step foot into something you can't see.

In order to maintain the ego, Ski decided not to tell Kenny anything about the incident at the Silver Club. Another party was now involved, but Kenny didn't need to know that. With all things considered, the usual successful outcome took place with the next game against the ten-point underdog New Hampshire. West Hartford won by thirty. The Boss too was overjoyed.

The next visit to the Silver Club was filled with nerves. However, this time was far different from the last visit. Ski not only received praise from the boss, but also a ten-thousand-dollar bonus for the tip that won Mike Dibella six figures.

Henceforth, the two bookmakers had begun a fruitful partnership to last for the next handful of years. Ski would continue to tip the boss on West Hartford games, but, by the last month of the season, only the victories were fixed.

Kenny had become well aware of his poor play by his disappointed teammates and coach.

As senior season was closing, the postseason was approaching, Kenny did not want to affect his draft status any worse. He told Ski he no longer would fix games starting the last week of the regular season.

"No more gambling!" Kenny said.

The damage was done though. The star did not realize he had already dropped to the second round according to scouts. Mostly, his poor performance against UConn and Buffalo hindered a top twenty pick.

Ski understood but was afraid to tell the Boss. Three conference championship games occurred without Dibella hearing a word from Ski. West Hartford would win all their tournament games, including their semifinal. Kenny was playing his best ball. They were to play in the conference finals against UConn. Kenny had a chance for redemption. He was not going to play poorly this time around.

The time had come. Ski gathered the courage to visit the club one afternoon where the Boss was a mainstay. Upon a pleasant greeting, he told the Boss that Kenny was out. "My best friend can no longer fix games; it will endanger his draft status."

The Boss unpredictably said to Ski, "No problem. It's a smart decision. I am more than satisfied with winning over a million. We must first look out for ourselves first, and then others after. Here take a load off. I'll bring you a drink."

Next, the two sat down for their first drink together ever. A white Russian wasn't the only thin the boss would hand to his new friend. A small black notepad was handed to Ski. In possession of the book, Mike rewarded Ski with the best clientele for any bookie in Hartford. A deal was made on the condition that Ski solely worked out of the Silver Club, which was no problem. The connection with the boss in time allowed Ski to network drugs and bets to anyone in Hartford by means of the Silver Club. Ski brought in a lot of new faces.

An awful performance for Kenny unfolded in the loss in the championship game to Uconn. Back in the condo that night, Ski slowly filled in Kenny with all the details of the Boss's involvement. Kenny didn't know what to think and assumed that everyone was connected to illegitimacy in Hartford somehow. He enjoyed playing the role.

Barely within a few months of establishing clientele from a new location, Ski would meet the most important men in Hartford at the Silver Club. One night in 1978, Ski met the man who would make him an easy hundred thousand in a year.

The owner of the entire World Jai Alai Association, Hal Coffey, would frequent the club. He first noticed it while prospecting the vacant building next door as a possible home for jai alai. The owner of World Jai Alai was new in town from Florida and he started sharing his plan to open ears immediately. Coffey made his way into the club one night. There he was discussing his motives with a Hartford police sergeant at the bar. Ski overheard the entire conversation as he sat one stool over. The great revenue that jai alai brought into Florida was revealed.

In the early 1970s, the jai-alai industry was trying to move north from its base in Florida. Connecticut became the first northern state to legalize gambling on jai alai, the fast-paced Basque game. In 1976, World Jai Alai [began] seeking a license to open a fronton in Hartford.[xxxii]

Thus, President Coffey became acquainted with Dibella. Coffey soon thereafter told the boss that jai alai would require a trustworthy house bookie who could "soften the books". The moment the Boss was asked if he could share a source, the Boss pointed toward Ski. He said to Coffey, "That's the best bookmaker around."

At the first encounter the two had in the club Ski explained the entire University of West Hartford scheme with the middle aged hefty president. Without delay, Coffey felt the NCAA scheme was the perfect experience for what could be manipulated within jai alai.

With acceptance, Coffey would next introduce Ski to Sergeant Pete Kendall, who told the young bookie that if he ever had trouble performing his job, "Come see me." The officer would make sure everything thing went properly until a certain point.

The first couple years of development went flawlessly. Games were sell-outs. Everyone looked Fabulous. Steve Martin played a gig at Hartford Jai Alai.

Chapter Sixteen: Hartford Jai Alai

Within three days of Pat moving into Hartford in 1980, Ski made arrangements in which Pat would try out in front of the president of World Jai Alai, Hal Coffey. Coffey was renting an apartment on Asylum Ave., keeping close to his number one prospect. The exclusive tryout went great. Pat volleyed against the main wall within Hartford Jai Alai mistake-free. He played every ball within the point marker on the sidewall. Coffey, the only spectator looked the teen up and down and then told Pat, "How are you this good? You are very talented—and American. But if this is to work, most importantly, if you are to succeed, listen to Ski. He sets everything up for me."

Pat did not know what all that meant at the time.

Pat, Kenny, and Ski met at Jenny's apartment the night of the tryout to celebrate. Pat told the other two what Coffey had said. "You're in," Ski then responded, "that's all it means."

Pat's dream had come true. He was so happy. Ski left after a couple of laughs and beers, as he didn't consume much ever, but Jenn and Kenny didn't have work. The three celebrated into the late night. Pat got very drunk. It was a good chemistry. Kenny could sense when someone didn't jive with his and Jenny's relationship, and Pat was all for their bond.

Pat's first game took place a week after the tryout. It did not go well. None of the games early in his first week went well. The game was much faster than it was against the barn, when there were no other players. Pat should have known, he had never played a full professional match before. His expectations coming in were the same as he had when he traveled to Grandpa Jacques house. However, the big show was far different.

From the first serve to start the game, Pat was lost. He continually blocked the other teams line to the ball on both the catch and return, which the judges ruled interference on five separate occasions. Pat was well aware from his previous lessons with Jacques that the ball must be caught and thrown in one continuous motion; yet, he could not contain his nerves, mishandling the ball several times. This would never happen against the barn. This poor play would continue into the double header the following day.

The inexperienced young man did notice that the other players seemed to be making blatant errors, almost as if they were acting.

Ski watched many of the games live in the stands to watch the script performed. He was there to see Pat's struggle. Obvious to all in attendance Pat's first night, he did not enjoy himself the least. Following the game, the instant Pat stepped out of the locker room Ski yanked his shoulder and pulled him aside. He told frustrated Pat, "We're going out for a drink!"

Settled in at the Silver Club, Ski explained, "Don't worry about being your best; if you mess up for me, others will mess up for you."

"What do you mean?"

"Pat, don't worry about playing your best. Pretend, it's like acting. That's what everyone else is doing."

"Really."

"I will tell you who is going to win, you make it happen-easy as that! I love this game because it's the fastest game on earth. And I can control it!"

"I'll give it a shot. I suck right now."

"If serving is your specialty, then do it. Easy enough!"

Pat excelled at the difficult skill, all because of Grandpa Jacques's time spent with the youth on the serve.

In jai alai, the server was to bounce the ball behind the serving line and then hurl the ball toward the front wall. Upon rebound the ball was to bounce between line four and seven on the side wall. If the serve didn't reach between four and seven the opposing team received the point. Pat, however, rarely gave up a point on one serve. It was pinpoint accuracy. Staying behind the opposition also reduced the interference calls.

Accordingly, he began to meet up with Ski before every game to determine the outcome of the game to come. A summary by Ski would include what all the other players intended to score and what Pat needed to score. The plan worked perfectly as Pat's serves played a major factor. The corruption Pat intermeshed quickly gained him the salary of a star, as well as a fan base that rooted for the lone American player. Every other player was known on a first name basis by the fans- Urquiaga, Roland, Gerny, Mendi, Jose, Said. Alongside all the fan favorites, Pat would look up at Ski in the stands once every match to wink and smile.

The popularity of the newly established gambling fix would influence many gambling addicts, but it too hosted a good night out in Hartford. Hence Ski and the jai alai gates took full advantage. The first months went perfect for Pat following Ski's advice. It was in 1981 when trouble appeared. The Adams downward spiral would return.

Pat thought Mark was out of his life forever. The brothers had not talked for nearly a year since he moved to Boston. Mark was living in south Boston, but he was not making wise decisions in the city at all. He talked to his mother for a while one night on the fact that he was ready to leave. She disclosed to Mark how Pat made the jai alai circuit. Mark was overtly shocked at how well his younger brother was doing.

Envy and fear facilitated Mark's decision to leave Boston for Hartford. Hartford was the only alternative to

Pittsfield. But Anna said, "No way," at the mention of his return, which was fine. Mark wanted to see what his baby brother got himself into and maybe mooch off Jenny, just as his brother had. If anything, Mark needed a temporary residence. He had no place to turn. Hartford only made sense. With no more of Russell's dope and a vast debt accumulated, no money needed for rent in Hartford sounded great. He therefore received Jenn's address from his mother, and, as simple as that, Mark headed straight for Hartford in February 1981.

He arrived on Fairfield Avenue when Pat was the only one home. It was quite an awkward scene after Pat walked down the stairs to check who rang the doorbell. There was his older brother standing there—the same brother he had not said more than ten words to in one conversation since their father had died. Subsequent to a moment of discomfort and a quick, sturdy handshake, the two walked upstairs.

Mark quickly sat down. Anxiously, he filled Pat in with the complete story of Boston.

"I fell into an impossible debt to Willy, the head up there. I had three choices: you 'either pay Willy, or you don't deal [at all], or you end up dead.'xxxiii Not only does Willy run south Boston through the South Hill Gang, but he works for the feds—I'm screwed. I need a place to hide out."

"I suppose you can stay here for a while if it's OK with Jenny. Are you in a lot of trouble, Mark?"

"I owe a lot of money." Mark took a deep breath.

"Just relax. We'll square this away," Pat said.

Jenn walked in at 10:00 p.m. from work with Marilyn, a co-worker who thought Pat was attractive. It was near three hours after Mark's arrival. Mark was sitting on her sofa, drinking a beer with Pat.

"Wow, it's a party! Hey, I know you," Jenn said.

"Yeah, I haven't seen you in a long time, Jenn."

"Both Adams boys. Great. This is Marilyn. Visiting Mark?"

Pat greeted the brunette with a broad smile.

"Kind of," Mark said, "Boston didn't work out—I was wondering if I could stay a few nights in Pat's room?"

"Gosh, no problem at all. You have the sofa out here too."

It was a huge nuisance for Pat, but it was his brother. Mark was especially bothersome this evening because Jenn knew that there was some chemistry between Pat and Marilyn, but Mark got in the way of any romantic implication.

After she finished handing out the first round of drinks, Jenn provided the blankets Mark would use on the floor in Pat's room. Following the laughs spawned by childhood recollections shared by all for a couple hours, Marilyn left Pat with a firm hug. With Kenny nowhere to be seen by two in the morning, it was bedtime for the Adams.

The two brothers shared a buzz as they laid five feet apart. Pat would then disclose his role in fixing jai alai games while the two brothers were attempting to fall asleep. Pat finished by telling Mark, "You are not to be involved at all or say a word."

Right after Pat told Mark to keep his mouth shut, Pat regretted telling his older brother. He knew something was going to come out of this exchange.

It was planned previous to Mark's arrival that Ski was to come over the next night, while Kenny and Jenn were at work and Pat had no games. The intention for their weekly meeting was to discuss the plan for the upcoming games. This meeting would be different. Mark was present when Ski arrived. Mark knew that Ski was the inside man from his brother's late night disclosure. The moment Ski arrived Mark could not keep his mouth shut.

"I'm Pat's brother, Mark. You must be Ski."

"Nice to meet you. You have a loyal brother." Ski smiled at Pat.

"I know. I'm very loyal too," Mark said. "I'm in a bit of a jam right now though. I had to fly out of Boston. I owe the

South Hill gang thirty grand right now- that drug business you know."

"I heard about that gang. He calls all the shots out of his garage. Doesn't that guy run everything up there- from placing bets to running drugs to cars—what's his name?"

"Willy."

"That's him. I heard he owns South Boston."

"Yeah. I actually think this scheme is right up his alley," Mark said.

"Your brother told you?" Ski asked.

"Yes, I won't tell a soul."

"The more people, the more problems," Ski said as he sinisterly stared at Pat sitting on the opposite sofa.

"Willy can invest a lot of money, but most important, he can get the feds on our side," Mark quickly replied.

"You're crazy," Ski said.

Mark leaned over and began to talk in a soft voice toward Ski. "I heard from many people on the street that Willy is an informant. He rats out people to get them off the street, so he can run everything. Trust me, the feds are going to figure this out. The more money you make the quicker they come. You need him on your side."

"Hmmm. I'll let you know—give us a minute. I got to talk to your brother about tomorrow."

The two would spend ten minutes in Pat's room. Surprising to Pat, Ski made no mention of what Mark brought up. It seemed to Pat as if the bookie was optimistic about the matter. He avoided showing any more distaste for unveiling the jai alai scheme. Pat's intuition was correct. Ski incessantly wanted to increase his underworld prestige. Before he left that night, he told Mark, "Talk to Willy for me."

Mark had no idea on his trip down to Hartford, fleeing a tremendous drug debt in Boston, he would return to Boston a week later with a proposal for Willy. Mark drove up to Boston the next winter morning following Ski's request. Ski gave no number or any way for Mark to reach him. Mark assumed Pat would let Ski know everything that would be discussed in Boston.

The meeting started rough for Mark, as it was made clear he was a joke. The meeting did finish smooth. Mark immediately called his brother after his discussion with Willy. He told Pat over the phone, "The South Hill gang would invest great funds into jai alai if the pre-results were shared with them!"

Pat thus shared this information with Ski. Upon Mark's return to Hartford that same day, Ski told Mark that he would accommodate Willy's request. Hartford Jai Alai now had the interest of the largest gang in Boston as well.

Russell Adams may have known what he was talking about.

Chapter Eighteen: The Dream's End

By 1982 Hartford Jai Alai was Connecticut's greatest adult attraction. The peak of jai alai was right in front of Pat Adams's eyes, in which he had unexpectedly become the main focal point of the sport. His fan base was huge. He especially enjoyed it, because he was the ace. Mistakes were planned for other players. Pat just had to make flawless serves, and that he did. The eight-hundred-person capacity complex was filled every game he played. Marilyn, Jenny, and Kenny joined Ski as spectators on the weekend when they weren't working next door. It was quite a loud and emotional atmosphere. Great wages were lost and won. The scheme was working perfectly.

Mark had to butt in, nonetheless. No problems escalated at first, even as Mark brought in such polarizing clientele through his Boston connection. It was after six months of a trial run that Ski finally told President Coffey what Mark, Pat Adams' brother, had set up.

At first impression the president paid no mind to it, but as soon as he heard that it was the South Hill Gang involved, he gave his full attention to Ski. A meeting was instantly set up with Mark. Coffey was 'a bear-like man with a bottomless wallet who [would] always be found at a table full of gangsters' at the Silver Club. He wanted to meet Willy. [xxxiv]

Three days subsequent to Mark and Coffey's discussion on Willy's expanded interest in jai alai, the two headed to meet the South Hill head at his office located on the back side of his South Boston "South Side Auto Shop". The three met in inside the small white office. Willy told Coffey, "I could make

Hartford Jai Alai a lot more money than what your baby bets are bringing in."

Coffey didn't hide his emotions. He was very interested, "How can we make a deal Willy?"

All clean-cut completely bald Willy did was hand Coffey a duffel bag with $100,000. Willy simply told Coffey, "Make me a profit." Willy was a man of a few words. He cut to the chase.

In leaving the garage, Mark was stopped. "Hey!" Willy, opening his shop door, looked at Mark and told him, "Your debts are cleared."

Consistent through the quiet ride, Mark kept a smile the entire way back to Hartford. It was the first time that he felt he had succeeded. His sole role in the scheme was to simply drive a briefcase of money back and forth from Hartford to Boston. He was trustworthy enough not to touch the money. He made out very well for his own needs in receiving substance with every commute.

The moment was now Mark's. Being the front runner for millions of dollars with out grief fed his ego full. In the empty bedroom on Fairfield Ave. he set-up shop, which was not much- Corduroys and blue jeans, flannels and Henley's.

With such residence, Mark utilized the hoop, which was still heavily used by the former pro. The most tumultuous, rowdy, revved up, late night games took place. Neighbors clued in on the loud obnoxious games under the lights, always after eleven. Mark never won a game of the hundred games in the year span. Mark was ever so frustrated, but only on the court. He was making Willy lots of money.

In the first year of Willy's involvement everyone profited favorably except for one important partner—Hartford Jai Alai. It became very obvious that there was a "siphoning of millions" out of Hartford Jai Alai. The vice president, named Mike Riley, who was always in a shirt and tie, had not been brought in on the scam. Riley, the man who held the accounting responsibilities for Hartford Jai Alai, could not figure why they were losing so much money. Great losses were clear as day in the quarter numbers, which seemed very strange to him. Jai alai was growing so popular in Hartford. As the bookkeeper, he was the only soul who discovered that there were huge substantial winners and minimal losers. Riley told Coffey in the president's office, "Something's not right here."

Things thus began to unravel rampantly. The vice president was just about the only one not committing any corruption in the Hartford Fronton. Riley received no support from Coffey upon his qualms, wherein his only option was to call the FBI. Jai Alai would quickly go out of business if they continued to lose in such a drastic way. It just didn't make any sense for VP Riley. He made the call for the FBI to perform an extensive internal audit.

Unfortunately for VP Riley, the FBI agent sent was also connected to Willy. The agent sent to investigate Hartford Jai Alai was Jack Palmer—a man who appeared just as any other agent. He had been in the FBI for twelve years, where he developed a reputation as Boston's top organized-crime investigator. The Feds put their best in the northeast on this case. Palmer, however, had a big secret.

There was a reason why Palmer requested this case during a briefing. The fed Jack Palmer and the gangster Willy Harrison went way back to childhood in south Boston. Palmer knew everything Willy was involved with since they were teens. Palmer became so successful as a fed all because he had a star informant who ran Boston. Palmer knew every move of Willy's, but never disclosed any little bit. The moment he heard Hartford Jai Alai at the precinct, he jumped out of his chair.

Whitey Harrison grew up next to Palmer in south Boston. They continued their friendship, as the two traveled toward opposite ends of the spectrum. Even though they conducted their labor in fields with different moral standards, they had a strong Southie bond. South Hill gangsters would provide Palmer with 'leads, [which] he would use to lock up Italian mafia members who competed with South Hill for control of Boston's rackets'[xxxv]. All the arrests Palmer made on mobsters made him appear as he was the best thing going. It was not known that Palmer turned a blind eye on all of Willy's deviance.

Palmer, actually, was Willy's most important informant. The instant Palmer heard the office mention bugging or surveillance on Willy's automobile shop, he would immediately contact his friend. That is exactly how Palmer got the jai alai case. He heard word of the investigation in the Boston office only days after he spoke with Willy about his new "Hartford Gig".

With Palmer's stature, a simple request made with administration was all it took for him to lead the case. The first step Palmer made into the jai alai investigation was to talk with President Coffey. Palmer knew Coffey knew Willy, but the President of Hartford Jai Alai didn't know to what extent Palmer knew Willy. Willy simply told Coffey, "Listen to Palmer, he'll make it all work."

Behind closed doors, Willy told Palmer, "Don't meet with President Coffey until three big winners are delivered." Soon thereafter the large purse, President and Fed would finally meet. Palmer told Coffey bluntly at the meeting that the president would face a grand jury if he did not shut Riley up. The president, however, could not move VP Riley. Riley lived a straightforward life. With an Air Force background, Riley was not budging. The lone attempt the president made of buying out Riley's contract failed. "I'm not selling out."

VP Riley would call Palmer every other day. Every conversation would conclude in a like manner. Riley would say, "Coffey is involved, I can feel it," or "He's trying to buy me out not to talk."

Palmer, seeing no resolution for Riley, told Coffey the problem had to be eliminated. The president would not let anything happen to Riley, however. In a phone call, the president made sure to tell Willy not to touch the VP. Willy did, though, hold a reputation throughout New England as a cold-blooded killer. Coffey knew this. A threat was made over the phone to call off the entire scheme, "If Riley's offed, this is all over!" But unfortunately, Riley had already spoken out too much.

VP Riley was a quick fix for the mob boss. Willy had one of his soldiers take care of the uneasy Riley. Days following Coffey's plea for Riley's life to Willy, Riley was shot point-blank in the face following a round of golf at Goodwin Park. The murder took place just down the street from Jenn's house. Things obviously became much tighter inside Hartford Jai Alai.

From the inside, Pat did not realize the degree to what he had taken part in- until Riley had been murdered. That night subsequent to the murder, Ski told Pat and Kenny, around the kitchen table, all the details he learned from the Boss of Riley's murder. A strong feeling of responsibility was felt within Pat, as Mark was in the middle of all of this. "I made this mess." Ski, however, told him not to feel guilty. The bookie put the situation in simple terms, "Just keep your mouth shut!"

The murder also brought Coffey to his breaking point. Coffey and Riley were childhood friends, and together they established ten successful frontons. Thenceforth, the Hartford police were now involved with the ordeal too, as the murder materialized within their jurisdiction. The once whispers of jai alai corruption had quickly become screams.

Police swept through the building interrogating everyone. Pat kept cool, but could sense others were speaking. He was not overly concerned though. Ski was his connection to corruption, and no one involved with the investigation knew of any guy named Ski.

Riley was well liked by everyone before he opened his mouth—he was honest and cared about others. He knew everyone's name and remembered specific things about the families and hobbies of others. The investigation of his murder was thorough. It was not full of loopholes, as Palmer's continued to be. The Hartford Police Department discovered that Coffey's personal bank account increased simultaneous to the decrease in the net income of Jai Alai. They knew the man they must pursue for the answers to Riley's murder was Coffey, the president himself.

Coffey withstood immense interrogation by the Hartford Police, yet still maintained his innocence. Meanwhile, Palmer was reassuring Willy that, with Riley gone, the feds didn't have a case. The Hartford detectives still continued to pry though. There was word inside the

Boston bureau from Palmer's peers that there was a connection between the South Hill Gang and Hartford Jai Alai.

Coffey kept quiet. Palmer kept quiet. The fed had the sense the dominos were beginning to fall. This mess couldn't be cleaned. He read a report titled "Hartford Jai Alai" from an undisclosed source when no other feds were in the office. It would indicate that Willy was involved. Thus, Palmer instantaneously contacted the gangster, as paranoia was beginning to set in.

Furthermore, the police uncovered the bookwork of the deceased VP Riley through a search warrant of Coffey's office. They compared it with the president's records. None of it matched up. Large sums of money were unaccounted for. The president was now trapped by the IRS, at least. Plea arrangements for Coffey had to be swiftly considered. How much jail time was he going to do? How much was he going to reveal.

Coffey chose to tell the Hartford police nearly everything. Palmer could not interfere with this interrogation or investigation at all. It was in the jurisdiction of the local police. The fed too didn't want to bring any unnecessary attention upon himself. Nonetheless, any opportunity he had to obtain information from the Hartford police he did. Consequently, he told Willy every little thing that he had heard on the investigation. The moment Palmer discovered that Coffey "gave up Willy" from a Hartford cop, he was on the phone with Willy.

President Coffey did not know that the worst thing he could have done was to snitch on Willy Harrison to avoid fraud conviction.

Mark, now staying in the other bedroom, got a call at Jenn's house one evening from a livid Willy. It was a quick phone call. Mark told his brother the details the second he hung up.

"I got called into Boston. I'm a dead man."

"What are you going to do?" Pat asked.

"I don't know. I have to get Willy out of this mess."

"Maybe you should see what he has to say."

"That's what I will do or he'll find me."

Mark left for Boston. When he returned to Hartford late that same evening, he was very quiet- quite different from his gregarious character. Pat attempted to open him up sarcastically. "So you're not dead."

Mark, on the contrary, didn't use words. He opened his coat and showed Pat a gun resting under his belt buckle.

"What's that for?" Pat asked.

"I have never used one of these before, but it is either I use it on Coffey, or Willy was going to use it on me."

Upon his return to Boston, Mark became well aware of the paranoia Palmer and Willy felt as he spoke with both of them privately at Palmer's house. There they would remind Mark of his great debt that had been rescinded. Also, the poor judgment Mark made to get South Hill involved in this dysfunction was brought forth. Mark had no other choice than to murder Coffey. Even so, it was difficult for Mark to carry the gun, let alone shoot it.

The plan for Mark had been scripted at Palmer's house, while the three sat at the fed's dining room table. Mark was to steal a car, wait outside Coffey's house secluded, and then follow Coffey in his Cadillac. At his destination, the moment Coffey got out of his car, Mark was to shoot him, quickly place the body in the trunk of the stolen car, and then dump him in a trash compactor. Next, he was to bring the car to a junk yard.

There were a couple of great flaws that developed with the plan. First, Mark stole a flashy mint Camaro to use in the murder, and he did not want to ruin it with blood. Second, he did not know where Coffey's destination was.

The day had arrived, however. Mark followed Coffey from his home in Farmington to the parking lot of Bradley International Airport. Upon arrival, in a thirty-second span, Hal Coffey was shot twice in the head and stuffed into the trunk of his own Cadillac. Mark left a dime on Coffey's chest, as instructed, which was a warning to anyone else who was going to rat out Willy.

President Coffey was intending to fly back to Florida. How appropriate it was that the exact time he was to leave Connecticut for good was the same time Mark was to carry out the plan to murder him. Accordingly, March 19th, 1982, Mark Adams assassinated the president of Jai Alai. However, it was no private matter. Many eyewitnesses came forth. Answers were sought.

As the blood and the body were discovered, arrests were inevitable. A picture of Coffey's body stuffed in his Cadillac's trunk made the front page of the *Courant*. Everyone involved with Hartford Jai Alai was again on edge. Indeed, all employees were assumed to be involved with Coffey's murder.

Mark, nonetheless, could not avoid being arrested. Five eyewitnesses saw him shoot Coffey in clear daylight, stuff the limp body in the Cadillac, and then speed away in a red Camaro. Massachusetts state police discovered the stolen car that afternoon, subsequent to the murder, driving on the Mass pike toward Boston. Mark was pulled over.

Even with the gun thrown from the car, Mark was still wearing the same clothes that he wore to stuff Coffey's body in the trunk. All dots were connected. The police saw he was still smeared in blood. The police notified Mark at the barracks that he fit the description of a murder suspect and that he must stay. He knew he had the right to an attorney and a phone call. It didn't take any longer than five minutes of questions before he broke down in the interrogation room and confessed. "Now I want my phone call."

Mark called Pat. Hours prior to the call, Pat was contacted by the fed Palmer. "If Mark avoids discussing my role with the murder, your brother won't get the death penalty.

Pat shared all this on the phone in simple terms with his brother without using names.

"Mark. What has happened?" Pat asked.

"Yeah I know. I did what I was supposed to. Everything has spun out of control," Mark said on the police barrack's phone.

"Listen. Keep it cool. The badge said you'll escape execution if you keep him out of it," Pat said.

"Tell 'em not to worry. I ain't saying nothing about him."

Mark took Pat's advice. The suspect ratted out Willy for a plea, not Palmer. The fed's would do anything to indict Willy. Their removal of the death penalty was all Mark needed to talk.

As brother of the suspect, Pat was obviously one of the first to be interviewed. He did not reveal anything though. He told the investigators, "I had no idea what my brother was into. I just wanted to play jai alai... He must have got in with the wrong people when he moved to Boston."

Ski was never questioned. Coffey loved the young man for his loyalty. The only proof of Ski's illegitimate connection existed in his own book. Ski made the president a lot of money through his creative fixing arrangements, but never asked for anything in return. It would be impossible to figure what Ski made knowing all the results.

Mob boss Willy Harrison was instantly sought after for his role in Coffey and Riley's murders. Mark would ultimately receive only a twenty-year murder sentence through his cooperation.

The fed Palmer has yet to be indicted, while Willy Harrison has yet to be caught.

It was difficult for Pat to take everything in, as it all happened so fast. He could do nothing for his brother, other than what Palmer told him to do. Mark had fallen into a far darker place than his father had.

The Silver Club continued running through all the corruption. Kenny would continue his entrepreneurial labor. Jenny, Kenny, and Pat continued to live together, until Kenny was caught with weed. It was an undercover agent who finally caught up to him in 1988.

With his good friend gone and a marriage proposal to Marilyn, Pat went back to Pittsfield with his fiancé. He bought the farm for a modest sum from his elderly grandfather and mother with the illegitimate earnings he had saved in a safe in Hartford. Grandpa Calvin and Anna Adams would remain on the farm for the duration of their lives.

Ski saved all his money throughout the years as well. Wisely, he got out of gambling and drugs immediately after the jai alai debacle. No one has seen or heard from the bookie since.

Correspondence would start day one of prison. A letter Kenny wrote to Pat from prison, a couple of months following his move back to Pittsfield, put everything into Kenny's perspective:

Dear Pat,

I ain't free no more. Tell you the truth I've never been free. Before I've become enslaved, I was an addict- a prisoner to substance. Now I'm imprisoned for simply being a street doctor. My crime- caught selling an herb to make others happy. A plant grown by nature has caused my incarceration and I'm doing a lot of time for this. The hypocrisy! All these big time hospitals are claiming their number one concern is pain. Our health system is most concerned with reducing patient's pain. Well, here is the super drug to reduce pain and bring hunger. Why not use it for its god given purpose? Or have we formed such a society where making money has taken precedent over the well being of the tax-paying citizen? Weed is the devil's drug they say, but here take these synthetic drugs for your pain. They may only give you seizures.

While I've been talking with other educated men in here, a gentleman by the name of Kevin White, from Virginia, told me what he had learned about weed. Come to find out, The Medical College of Virginia did a study in 1974 that concluded THC slowed lung and breast cancer, and virus-induced leukemia in mice. The government knows this. Reagan and Bush tried to have universities repress all their beneficial marijuana research. They make weed appear to be a tool of the devil. The war on drugs! Don't get me wrong, the shit I got hooked on is no good, but I need help not enslavement. There ain't no second chance in here.

Think of jai alai Pat, we know very well of a federal agent who got away with planning a murder. What kind of backward world do we live in? If we look much deeper into this society, our leaders, our presidents, are responsible for framing wars in which thousands of innocent die.

And these wily acts are all for individual prosperity. They ain't making me freer, if anything war makes the citizen pay more into a never-ending debt. I can honestly say my crime is not one of greed. Sure it brings me some money in the pockets, but, more so, I enjoy sharing something with an individual that will bring them a pleasure not affecting anyone but that person. I'm here for ten years because of a drug less harmful than cigarettes.

Sharing some pleasure has gotten me enslaved. Now I am giving my employment to the state for free. All I am is a statistic- A Black Man In Jail! I get arrested for selling a drug celebrating happiness and peace, yet rulers were provided riches and land through the extermination of peaceful cultures.

Hartford will never be a peaceful city man. It lost any chance the day we hosted the Hartford Convention. The War of 1812 is so significant because it advanced the most evil of trends. We saw a government use false pretense to justify a war in order to accomplish the expansionist nature. Impressment was the justification, but conquering the west was the true motive. The war furthered this developing policy, but the New England Federalists briefly checked and balanced the total surrender of our rights to the government. Now, there are no longer any Federalists left who seek true justice, just men accumulating their very own pot of gold.

Those Federalists knew the importance of a consistent domestic policy. Yet, as the war illustrated, we have become so concerned with exterior conflict that we lose control within. Thus the internal struggle strengthens.

These men we have elected through the years cannot tap into the minds great tool of creativity. The nature of our government makes this so. Policies and wars are already calculated. There's no debate. When man becomes a statistic and controlled like a robot, his leaders themselves become robots. Hence, robots have no passion, no foresight, and no creativity. No place in a democracy![xxxvi]

Wars of today are of the most frightening manner—lies promote expansion and disrupt self-sustaining communities. Destructive motives are put in place that foster individual benefit. Why are private military contracts made prior to war?

Yes, our leaders predetermine death and are still claimed as legends. I sell herb and am a slave. But it's all about the money. We are capitalist. Everything is based on profit. Making more money through unnecessary expansion takes precedent over the improvement of our slums.

Government has become the regulator for our capitalism, while I, on the other hand, am a non-factor with no role, except to expand the corrections system. It is the 'Atomic

Energy Commission that is the largest industrial enterprise in the United States', that enterprise creates contracts with the armament industry. Yes, it's owned privately, but the armament industry produces the massive amounts of weapons in accordance to plans made by the state. Sadly, our plans are based on arms production, which means we must use them from time to time. There is no interest in changing our ways to develop an economy based on peace and energy rather than war.

The common man is just as enslaved as me, just a cog in this war machine. His individual prestige holds no importance within our capitalism—he is expendable. These industries have eliminated ownership of the product produced, now that bureaucracy has complete oversight. Thus, there no longer exists "individual initiative, daring, or risk-taking." Our new leaders "lack individuality and imagination. The giant corporations, which control the economic-and to a large degree the political-destiny of the country, constitute the very opposite of the democratic process; they represent power without control by those whom they rule."[xxxvii]

We have no power. It has become one nation under corporations. Madison put the country in jeopardy of losing its independence and never was held accountable. I sold someone weed, and I am locked up for years. "The friends of war will never make peace; that tree does not produce such fruit. If we wish for peace, let us be reasonable; let the friends of peace be employed to make it. We must change our rulers; we must elect no more such men as they are, and we shall again be happy."[xxxviii] *We must consider what Martin Luther King said, "A nation that continues year after year to spend more money on military defense than on programs of social uplift is approaching spiritual death."*[xxxix]

Finally, Pat, we need to find "a new world, in the sense, that so many of us seem to have forgotten in this day of rocket ships and atom bombs, that our last opportunity for oncoming generations to create a society of peace and harmony in a world of hate and suspicion"[xl] *depends on changing this country's purpose. The foundation of our democracy has been long cracked as a result of the manipulation of the truth. We can begin to avoid additional damage to our foundation by* eliminating falsehood. As Martin Luther King said, "If there is to be peace on earth and good will toward men, we must finally believe in the ultimate morality of the universe, and believe that all reality hinges on moral foundations."[xli]

Keep breathing,

Kenny

[i] *History of Hartford County*, Charles Burpee, 1928, pg. 44.
[ii] *The Examiner*, Barent Gardenier, 1814, pg. 98.
[iii] *History of the People of the United States, Volume 3*, John Bach McMaster, pgs. 242–243.
[iv] Ibid., pg. 243.
[v] *The Naval War of 1812*, Theodore Roosevelt, pg. 21.
[vi] Ibid., pg. 21.
[vii] Ibid., pgs. 22–23.
[viii] Gardenier, pg. 5.
[ix] Ibid., pg. 23.
[x] *Expansionists of 1812*, Julius W. Pratt, 1957, pg. 37.
[xi] Ibid., pg. 149.
[xii] Ibid., pg. 131.
[xiii] Ibid., pg. 157.
[xiv] Ibid., pg. 161.
[xv] *A History of the People of the United States*, John Bach McMaster, pg. 550.
[xvi] Ibid., pgs. 543–544.
[xvii] War on the Detroit: The Capitulation by an Ohio Vounteer, Edited by Milo Milton Quaife, 1940, 282-305
[xviii] Ibid., pg. 192.
[xix] Ibid., pg. 73.
[xx] Ibid., pg. 6.
[xxi] Ibid., pg. 372.
[xxii] *The War of 1812*, Henry Adams, pg. 279.
[xxiii] *Epochs of American History, Formation of the Union*, Albert Bushnell Hart, 1893, pg. 215.
[xxiv] Ibid., pg. 215.
[xxv] *The First American: The Life and Times of Benjamin Franklin*, H. W. Brands, 2000, pg. 123.
[xxvi] *Amateurs to Arms*, John R. Elting, pg.7.
[xxvii] Gardenier, pg. 72.
[xxviii] *History of the Hartford Convention*, Theodore Dwight, 1833, pg. 413.
[xxix] Gardenier, pg. 259.
[xxx] Dwight, pg. 417.
[xxxi] Gardenier, pg. 289.
[xxxii] *The Harford Courant*: "Former FBI Agent Indicted in Killing," Edmund Mahoney, A1, May 5, 2005.
[xxxiii] *Black Mass*, Lehr & O'Neill, pg. 183.
[xxxiv] Mahoney, A1.
[xxxv] Ibid.

[xxxvi] *May Man Prevail? An Inquiry into the Facts and Fictions of Foreign Policy*, Erich Fromm, pg. 79, 1964.

[xxxvii] Fromm, pg. 78–79.

[xxxviii] Gardenier, pg. 83.

[xxxix] *The Words of Martin Luther King Jr.*, 1987, pg. 87.

[xl] *The Pan American: Mexican Oil Refinery*, Flint, back cover, 1946.

[xli] *The Words of Martin Luther King Jr.*, 1987, pg. 72.

47017439R00142

Made in the USA
Middletown, DE
14 August 2017